the
MASS
MEDIA

OPPOSING VIEWPOINTS®

Other Books of Related Interest in the Opposing Viewpoints Series:

Censorship
Chemical Dependency
Drug Abuse
Sexual Values
Terrorism

Additional Books in the Opposing Viewpoints Series:

Abortion
AIDS
American Foreign Policy
American Government
The American Military
American Values
America's Prisons
The Arms Race
Biomedical Ethics
Central America
Constructing a Life Philosophy
Crime & Criminals
Criminal Justice
Death and Dying
The Death Penalty
Economics in America
The Environmental Crisis
Latin America
Male/Female Roles
The Middle East
Nuclear War
The Political Spectrum
Problems of Africa
Social Justice
The Soviet Union
The Vietnam War
War and Human Nature

the MASS MEDIA

OPPOSING VIEWPOINTS®

David L. Bender & Bruno Leone, *Series Editors*

Neal Bernards, *Book Editor*

Thomas Modl, *Assistant Editor*

OPPOSING VIEWPOINTS SERIES ®

Greenhaven Press   577 Shoreview Park Road   St. Paul, Minnesota 55126

Library of Congress Cataloging-in-Publication Data

The Mass media.

   (Opposing viewpoints series)
   Bibliography: p.
   Includes index.
   1. Mass media—United States.   I. Bernards, Neal,
1963-   . II. Modl, Tom, 1963-   . III. Series.
P92.U5M277   1988   302.2'34'0973   87-14848
ISBN   0-89908-425-7
ISBN   0-89908-400-1 (pbk.)

"Congress shall make no law . . . abridging the freedom of speech, or of the press."

First Amendment to the US Constitution

The basic foundation of our democracy is the first amendment guarantee of freedom of expression. The *Opposing Viewpoints Series* is dedicated to the concept of this basic freedom and the idea that it is more important to practice it than to enshrine it.

Contents

Chapter 5: Is Advertising Harmful to Society?

Why Consider Opposing Viewpoints?

"It is better to debate a question without settling it than to settle a question without debating it."

Joseph Joubert (1754-1824)

The Importance of Examining Opposing Viewpoints

The purpose of the Opposing Viewpoints books, and this book in particular, is to present balanced, and often difficult to find, opposing points of view on complex and sensitive issues.

Probably the best way to become informed is to analyze the positions of those who are regarded as experts and well studied on issues. It is important to consider every variety of opinion in an attempt to determine the truth. Opinions from the mainstream of society should be examined. But also important are opinions that are considered radical, reactionary, or minority as well as those stigmatized by some other uncomplimentary label. An important lesson of history is the eventual acceptance of many unpopular and even despised opinions. The ideas of Socrates, Jesus, and Galileo are good examples of this.

Readers will approach this book with their own opinions on the issues debated within it. However, to have a good grasp of one's own viewpoint, it is necessary to understand the arguments of those with whom one disagrees. It can be said that those who do not completely understand their adversary's point of view do not fully understand their own.

A persuasive case for considering opposing viewpoints has been presented by John Stuart Mill in his work *On Liberty*. When examining controversial issues it may be helpful to reflect on this suggestion:

> The only way in which a human being can make some approach to knowing the whole of a subject, is by hearing what can be said about it by persons of every variety of opinion, and studying all modes in which it can be looked at by every character of mind. No wise man ever acquired his wisdom in any mode but this.

Analyzing Sources of Information

The Opposing Viewpoints books include diverse materials taken from magazines, journals, books, and newspapers, as well as statements and position papers from a wide range of individuals, organizations and governments. This broad spectrum of sources helps to develop patterns of thinking which are open to the consideration of a variety of opinions.

Pitfalls To Avoid

A pitfall to avoid in considering opposing points of view is that of regarding one's own opinion as being common sense and the most rational stance and the point of view of others as being only opinion and naturally wrong. It may be that another's opinion is correct and one's own is in error.

Another pitfall to avoid is that of closing one's mind to the opinions of those with whom one disagrees. The best way to approach a dialogue is to make one's primary purpose that of understanding the mind and arguments of the other person and not that of enlightening him or her with one's own solutions. More can be learned by listening than speaking.

It is my hope that after reading this book the reader will have a deeper understanding of the issues debated and will appreciate the complexity of even seemingly simple issues on which good and honest people disagree. This awareness is particularly important in a democratic society such as ours where people enter into public debate to determine the common good. Those with whom one disagrees should not necessarily be regarded as enemies, but perhaps simply as people who suggest different paths to a common goal.

Developing Basic Reading and Thinking Skills

In this book carefully edited opposing viewpoints are purposely placed back to back to create a running debate; each viewpoint is preceded by a short quotation that best expresses the author's main argument. This format instantly plunges the reader into the midst of a controversial issue and greatly aids that reader in mastering the basic skill of recognizing an author's point of view.

A number of basic skills for critical thinking are practiced in the activities that appear throughout the books in the series. Some of the skills are:

Evaluating Sources of Information   The ability to choose from among alternative sources the most reliable and accurate source in relation to a given subject.

Separating Fact from Opinion   The ability to make the basic distinction between factual statements (those that can be demonstrated or verified empirically) and statements of opinion (those that are beliefs or attitudes that cannot be proved).

Identifying Stereotypes   The ability to identify oversimplified, exaggerated descriptions (favorable or unfavorable) about people and insulting statements about racial, religious or national groups, based upon misinformation or lack of information.

Recognizing Ethnocentrism   The ability to recognize attitudes or opinions that express the view that one's own race, culture, or group is inherently superior, or those attitudes that judge another culture or group in terms of one's own.

It is important to consider opposing viewpoints and equally important to be able to critically analyze those viewpoints. The activities in this book are designed to help the reader master these thinking skills. Statements are taken from the book's viewpoints and the reader is asked to analyze them. This technique aids the reader in developing skills that not only can be applied to the viewpoints in this book, but also to situations where opinionated spokespersons comment on controversial issues. Although the activities are helpful to the solitary reader, they are most useful when the reader can benefit from the interaction of group discussion.

Using this book and others in the series should help readers develop basic reading and thinking skills. These skills should improve the readers' ability to understand what they read. Readers should be better able to separate fact from opinion, substance from rhetoric and become better consumers of information in our media-centered culture.

This volume of the Opposing Viewpoints books does not advocate a particular point of view. Quite the contrary! The very nature of the book leaves it to the reader to formulate the opinions he or she finds most suitable. My purpose as publisher is to see that this is made possible by offering a wide range of viewpoints which are fairly presented.

David L. Bender
Publisher

Introduction

"The agencies (of mass communication) can advance the progress of civilization or they can thwart it."

Commission on Freedom of the Press, 1947.

In today's informational society, the public avidly consumes the mass media's messages while often remaining oblivious to their effects. The average citizen consumes scores of media-produced images each day, yet rarely considers their impact.

Some analysts criticize the media for being too influential and pervasive, but supporters say mass media serve only as simple tools of communication. No matter which side is correct, the media's role in American culture needs to be periodically evaluated.

Jerry Falwell's *Liberty Report*, an evangelical publication, blames the media's content for a deterioration in American morals. Prior to radio and television, Falwell and other religious leaders say, parents could control their children's environment. With cable television, CD players, and FM radio, parents must compete with rock stars, TV actors, and movie idols for their children's values development. According to some religious leaders, these media stars promote non-traditional values that are detrimental to family living and moral lifestyles.

Media defenders believe the media do not have a negative impact. They argue that people view the fantasy-world of mass media, especially television, as a cathartic outlet for their aggressions, not as a representation of reality. They point out that most citizens are not sociopaths though they may view thousands of rapes and murders on television. And, they contend, even if the media potentially have a negative influence, they have only as much power as the public allows. Viewers can choose to turn off their televisions and subscribers can read other newspapers. The media exist only to entertain and inform the public, not to change them.

In contrast, many political scientists argue that the media do change society, altering politics, for example, by promoting certain issues and candidates and neglecting others. Critics claim the media maliciously destroyed former Senator Gary Hart's chance to become the 1988 Democratic presidential nominee by publicizing his alleged extra-marital affairs. Hart renounced his candidacy shortly after the *Miami Herald* published a story detailing his weekend in Washington with a fashion model. The *Herald's* decision to probe Hart's personal life rather than focus exclusively on his political views created a great deal of controversy. Many argue that even popular presidents such as John F. Kennedy could not have survived similar scrutiny by the media.

Just as critics say the media destroyed Hart, others contend that the media "made" President Reagan. His confident answers and calm demeanor in the face of media criticism reassured the nation that he controlled the presidency. Even when Reagan quoted statistics incorrectly or made gaffes during debates, the public forgave him. To critics, it appeared that the more Reagan stumbled, the more his popularity soared. Americans, cynics said, could forgive an incompetent president if he had an amiable, trustworthy media image. However, should a president sincerely strive to do right but perform poorly in the media, the public would not be so tolerant.

To fully understand the mass media's impact on society, consumers must critically examine the material they read, see, and hear: Why is a certain story considered newsworthy? What is an ad really trying to sell? What motivates a politician to action?

The range of opinions in *The Mass Media: Opposing Viewpoints* considers the question of mass media's effect on society. The five topics debated are: Are the Media Biased? Should Government Regulate the Media? What Influence Do the Media Have on Society? How Do the Media Affect Politics? and Is Advertising Harmful to Society? The authors included in this anthology are politicians, journalists, religious leaders, sociologists, and experts in mass communication. Their arguments will help the reader understand the complexities inherent in any debate on the mass media's impact. But more importantly, their arguments underscore the obvious; namely, that no simple and formulaic conclusions are readily available.

Are the Media Biased?

the MASS MEDIA

Chapter Preface

Few people working in the national news media claim that the media give a perfectly objective and unbiased portrayal of events. Even the most sincerely objective reporters and editors express bias simply by choosing what facts to include and what to leave out when writing news stories. But is this bias always a product of individual judgment, or do the national media have an institutional bias that consistently distorts their reporting? And does this bias seriously hinder the credibility of the news?

Some critics do see a consistent bias in the news coverage by the national media. Many conservatives view the major news services and television networks as an arrogant, liberal elite, more interested in advancing their own influence on society than in promoting the good of the nation. Some left-wing critics point to the control of the major media by a shrinking circle of large corporations. They argue that the media distort the news to protect the interests of their corporate owners and government allies. Still other media observers who don't see a *conscious* conspiracy to distort the news believe the national media unintentionally bias their coverage in favor of government officials and policies. These observers point out that much of what the national media report as news involves government officials and often uses information provided by the government. They argue that the national media provide too much of a forum for government officials and do too little independent investigating and reporting.

Defenders of the national news media argue that claims of significant distortion of the news are exaggerated. Although admitting that the media rely on government officials for much of their information, they respond that it is the reporters and editors who decide how this information is presented. They also insist that even though reporters have their own views about what they are covering, most reporters consider it their professional responsibility to try to give all sides a fair hearing. Many in the media dismiss charges of distorting or controlling the news by claiming that there are many different viewpoints available to the interested news consumer. They point to the wide variety of publications focusing on public affairs and the availability of air time for alternative views through access to cable television. In fact, some argue that the national media's control of the news is declining, not increasing.

The viewpoints in this chapter debate the nature and effect of bias in the news.

"The content of news is a more or less faithful reflection of affairs as they are understood by the persons engaged in them."

Objective Reporting Is Responsible

Paul H. Weaver

Reporters who claim to be objective are often criticized by some as merely hiding a bias toward the status quo. In the following viewpoint, Paul H. Weaver, a former associate editor of *Public Interest* and *Fortune*, defends the reporting methods of journalists covering the government and other social leaders. He also argues that because of the large amount of information available, reporters maintain their independence and their responsibility to the public through their ability to choose what to report. In spite of having been written more than a decade ago, it remains a relevant argument for objective journalism.

As you read, consider the following questions:

1. What are some of the advantages, according to the author, of a reporter having access to government officials and other important figures?
2. Why does Weaver think that news gathered by the press in the traditional way is intelligible to the average citizen?
3. What disadvantages does the author see in the media abandoning its traditional cooperation with political leaders?

Reprinted with permission of the author from THE PUBLIC INTEREST, No. 35 (Spring, 1974), pp. 67-88. Copyright © 1974 by National Affairs Inc.

Traditionally, American journalism has been very close to, dependent upon, and cooperative with, official sources. This has been one of its problems, but it has also been its greatest strength and virtue. For in various ways this arrangement has maximized both the openness and flexibility of American government and the amount of information available to the citizenry. However, a small but significant and still-growing segment of the journalistic community has begun to revise this relationship by assuming a posture of greater independence and less cooperativeness. They see this change as a modest reform which will render American journalism purer, better, and truer to its traditional aspirations. In fact, it represents a radical change. In the long run it could make the press "freer" but also less informative and possibly more partisan; and this in turn could make the political system more closed, less flexible, and less competent.

To appreciate the meaning of what has happened, we may begin with the simple fact that journalism is the enterprise of publishing a current account of events. As such, it cannot proceed until three prior questions have been settled. First, there is the question of how, where, and on what basis to find and validate information. Second, there is the question of the point of view from which events are to be surveyed and characterized. And third, there is the question of the audience to be addressed and the basis on which it is to be aggregated. Abstractly, one can imagine any number of possible resolutions of these issues, but in practice things work out more simply. For wherever one looks in the modern world, daily journalism seems to assume one of two general forms: the partisan and the liberal.

Two Kinds of Journalism

Partisan journalism, which prevails in many European countries, and which has traditionally been represented in the United States by the "journal of opinion" rather than the newspaper, begins with an explicitly political point of view. It is ideological journalism. It aims at assembling an audience that shares its point of view; its object is to interpret public affairs from within that point of view; and it gathers information for the purpose of illuminating and particularizing such interpretation. Such a journalism is less concerned with information as such than with the maintenance and elaboration of its point of view. To it, events are more interesting for the light they cast on its "position" than for what they are, or seem, on their face.

Liberal journalism, by contrast, which prevails in the English-speaking world, is characterized by a preoccupation with facts and events as such, and by an indifference to—indeed, a systematic effort to avoid—an explicitly ideological point of view. It aims instead at appealing to a universal audience on the basis of its non-

18

political, "objective" point of view and its commitment to finding and reporting only "facts" as distinct from "opinion." Liberal journalism strives to be a kind of *tabula rasa* [clean state] upon which unfolding events and emerging information inscribe themselves. Its principal concern is to find as many events and as much information as it can, and it does this by going to "sources"—persons and organizations directly involved in the events, upon whom it relies both for information and for the validation of this information.

Striving To Be Objective

Most journalists fully realize that objective methods provide no guidelines for the selection either of stories or of which facts go into stories. Nevertheless, in making the selection, journalists strive to be objective, both in intent, by applying personal detachment; and in effect, by disregarding the implications of the news. They do not choose the news on the basis of whom it will help or hurt; and when they cannot ignore implications, they try to be fair.

Herbert Gans, *Deciding What's News*, 1979.

Throughout the 20th century, American journalism has been solidly in the liberal camp. It has sought a universal audience rather than a factional one; its central objective has been to find and publish as much information about as many events as quickly as possible; and it has striven to do this on the basis of a non-partisan, non-political, "facts-only" point of view. Or at least these have been its ideals; the extent of their actual realization has been subject, not only to the vicissitudes of human judgment, but also to two tensions inherent in the very idea of a liberal journalism.

Inherent Tensions

The first of these is the tension between access and autonomy, between the effort of the press to get as much unambiguously true information about as many events as possible—which requires a maximum of access to the actors in these events, which in turn entails a maximum of dependency on these actors—and its effort to preserve its capacity for independent judgment. The second tension arises out of the desire of liberal journalists to avoid taking a political point of view, which conflicts with the inevitability that, in the course of describing events, some sort of point of view will be assumed (observation and writing cannot proceed in the absence of one), and that no point of view will ever be totally devoid of political implications.

To these complex problems, the established liberal tradition of American journalism provides a suitably complex resolution. As between access and autonomy, the tradition opts massively and with a clear conscience for access. This choice is reflected not only in the way newsmen go about their work, but in almost every other feature of American journalism as well, from the form of the news story to the role of the newspaper owner. By opting for access, the American press has given priority and reality to its ideals of acting as a *tabula rasa* and maximizing the amount of raw information it provides to the electorate. This same emphasis on access also goes a long way toward settling, if only unintentionally, the problem of point of view. A *tabula rasa* that is written on primarily by persons involved in events inevitably reflects their slant on the world.

In practice, then, this emphasis on access means the following:

First, virtually all the information published by the press is derived from (and is validated by) "high-level sources," i.e., persons, officials, and organizations actively involved in the events in question.

Second, what newsmen know about the events and issues they cover, and about the general context in which these occur, they acquire almost exclusively from the persons involved rather than from external professional, academic, or ideological sources and authorities.

Third, the point of view from which newsmen write is largely determined by the views, concerns, vocabularies, and situations of those actually involved in public affairs. The viewpoint of the American press is thus a practical rather than ideological or theoretical one.

And fourth, as a result of this emphasis on access, newsmen are routinely aware of—or can easily gather—a truly immense amount of information. They are authentic ringside observers of men and events. They can never publish more than a small fraction of what they know (or have reason to believe), and what they do publish is backed up by a large, if often unarticulated, familiarity with the persons, institutions, and issues involved.

The Power To Choose

Yet if the "objective" tradition defines American journalism as a primarily derivative and dependent enterprise, it also provides the newsman with a limited but still quite important sphere of independence. Partly this independence has existed by virtue of the sheer volume of events and information which are routinely available to the working newsman. He therefore is confronted with the daily and hourly necessity of choosing, and to choose is to exercise a measure of independent power. This power is enhanced by the fragmentation and indiscipline of American government. Not only do they increase the number of points of access for the newsmen seeking a given bit of information, but they also create for him the opportunity—often exploited in practice—to follow the maxim *divide et impera* [divide and conquer], an approach whose utility is made much greater by the almost insatiable appetite of most officials for the two political resources which the newsman possesses automatically: publicity and information. The traditional journalist, then, is not utterly at the mercy of his sources.

A Lamentable Retreat

If newspapers were to abandon the goal of an unbiased news report and become organs of advocacy and opinion like *National Review* and *The New Republic*, they might well forfeit an important part of their function. They would not be as readily recognized as impartial proxy for the public in scrutinizing the sources of power in society. . . .

Readers would be left to piece together an approximate picture of reality by ranging across the spectrum of opinion journals and striking an average from their various versions of "news.". . .

It would be a sharp and lamentable retreat from the concept of responsible and undistorted journalism that has been developed in this country through the generations.

John Hulteng, *Playing It Straight*, 1981.

Just as important as the fact of the newsman's power is the independent way in which the liberal tradition of American journalism has encouraged him to use that power. To begin with, the tradition demands that the newsman maintain a strict formal independence of his sources: There are to be no financial conflicts of interest, and excessively close personal or ideological relationships are frowned upon. Second, each of the newsman's uses of his selective power is subject to a process of review by his journalistic peers and superiors; not only is the newsman supposed to be free of obligations to his sources, but also he is held answerable before the court of journalistic opinion. Third and most important, there is the traditional norm of "independent" judgment. The newsman is not to have a single, comprehensive, ideological point of view, but the liberal tradition of American journalism does encourage him to have an occasional *ad hoc* opinion and to bring such views to bear in his reporting—provided they pass muster with his journalistic colleagues and superiors, and provided also that there aren't many such opinions and that they manifest themselves only infrequently. (James Reston is an exemplar of this ethos, a man of judgment rather than a man of partisan ideology.) And as vehicles for the expression of these modest and occasional opinions, the liberal tradition sanctions, in addition to "objective" reporting, the devices of muckraking and the "crusade" against a particular instance of inequity. These latter are not often used, but they do remain in the newsman's arsenal to define alternative modes of dealing with institutions and events—and to give the newsman further room for exercising independent judgment. . . .

Intelligible News

The great virtue of the liberal tradition of American journalism is that it enables the press to find and print a great deal of information—much more of it, and more quickly, than partisan newspapers can. For the newsman, it has the further advantage of affording him an opportunity to become truly learned and sophisticated about public affairs through an informal process of close personal observation. And for the citizen it has the virtue that it produces news which is generally intelligible. One can know that the content of news is a more or less faithful reflection of affairs as they are understood by the persons engaged in them, or at least as officialdom as a whole sees them. What is more, the general perspective on events is a practical one. News, presented in this way, is sensitive to the practitioner's questions of "What next?" and "How to?" and "Who are my friends and enemies?"— and this in turn increases the possibilities that public opinion, reacting to the news, will have significant impact on the day-to-day conduct of government.

Of course, the established tradition has its shortcomings as well, and some of them are quite severe. It is a kind of journalism that is very easily (and very often) manipulated, especially by government but also by newsmen themselves. In any particular instance, the reader can never be absolutely sure that the impression being conveyed to him is a reasonably accurate reflection of the reality of affairs. And beyond that, traditional liberal journalism is perhaps excessively controlled by the ethos and conventional wisdom prevailing among "insiders" and shared by newsmen. In short, the "objective" tradition has the vices and virtues inherent in the idea of acting as a *tabula rasa*. But the virtues are substantial ones too, and the vices, serious though they are, are to no small extent inherent in the very mission of journalism as defined by the liberal tradition: publishing a current account of current events for "the general reader," i.e., the ordinary citizen. . . .

Partisan Journalism

Now the partisan mode of journalism has its virtues. It does not evade the problem of "point of view" as liberal journalism does, and in this sense it has an appealing honesty. It also has the capacity to create and sustain coherent bodies of political opinion; at a time when political opinion in this country so often [is] contradictory and inchoate, that is a very important trait. This is why "journals of opinion," existing on the margins of American journalism, have been so important and desirable.

But if, over the long run, American journalism were ever to turn massively to the partisan mode, the consequences of this development would extend to nearly every aspect of our political system. Partisan journalism would not increase the openness of the system, it would sharply decrease it. It would not reduce the scope of political conflict, but enlarge it. It would not increase the capacity of American government to act effectively and flexibly in meeting emergent needs, but would tend to paralyze it. It would not empower public opinion as a whole, but would transform it into a congeries of rigid ideological factions eternally at war with one another and subject to the leadership of small coteries of ideologues and manipulators. Indeed, it would tend to transform the entire nature of American politics: From having been a popular government based on a flexible consensus, it would become Europeanized into a popular government based on an equilibrium of hostile parties and unchanging ideologies.

The alternative to such a "Europeanization" of journalism and politics, it should be emphasized, does not have to be a massive and uncritical reversion to the way things were during the 1950's and early 1960's. Even if this were possible—which it isn't—it would clearly be undesirable. Both officialdom and the press were then busily abusing the "objective" tradition, officialdom by treating the media as an institution to be deliberately "managed" for its own expediential purposes, and the press by encouraging and acquiescing in these efforts out of inertia and a generalized avidity to print "big news" as often and as easily as possible.

Curb Abuses

There are ways to curb these abuses while still preserving the benefits of the liberal tradition of our press which the "adversary" approach would squander. Government can increase the amount of information which is formally made available on the public record. It can scale down its "public relations" operations to the point where they cannot easily operate as instruments of press management and are content instead merely to disseminate information. As Joseph Lee Auspitz and Clifford W. Brown, Jr., have suggested, the "strategic" cast of mind giving rise to, among other things, the habit of "managing" the press for purposes of personal power can be discouraged by strengthening the political party, which embeds individual actors in an institutional context, channels and restrains their ambition, and promotes a "representative" as against a "strategic" ethos. And the press, for its own part, can help recover the objective tradition by abandoning its flirtation with the "oppositional" posture and by ceasing to exploit public affairs for their sensation value (since the desire to exploit public affairs in this way is the main incentive leading the press to acquiesce in the manipulations of "strategically"-minded officials). The result, I believe, will be a journalism that provides more, and more useful, information to the citizenry, and a political system that, in consequence, comes a bit closer than in the past to realizing its historic ideals.

"Objectivity in journalism effectively erodes the very foundation on which rests a responsible press."

Objective Reporting Is Irresponsible

Theodore Glasser

Over the years "rules of objectivity" have evolved to help journalists keep their biases out of their reports. But in the following viewpoint, Theodore Glasser, a journalism professor at the University of Minnesota, states that not only does this "objective" style of reporting actually promote a bias toward the status quo, it keeps reporters from taking responsibility for what they report.

As you read, consider the following questions:

1. According to Glasser, what is the significance of the *Edwards* case in defining a reporter's responsibility?
2. Glasser thinks that it is unfortunate that reporters are often only translators of the views of officials. Yet in the previous viewpoint, Paul Weaver sees this as one of the strengths of American journalism. With whom do you agree? Why?
3. Why, according to the author, should reporters be more concerned with the consequences of their reporting? What must change before they will be?

Theodore Glasser, "Objectivity Precludes Responsibility," *The Quill*, February 1984. Reprinted with the author's permission.

By objectivity I mean a particular view of journalism and the press, a frame of reference used by journalists to orient themselves in the newsroom and in the community. By objectivity I mean, to a degree, ideology; where ideology is defined as a set of beliefs that function as the journalist's "claim to action."

As a set of beliefs, objectivity appears to be rooted in a positivist view of the world, an enduring commitment to the supremacy of observable and retrievable facts. This commitment, in turn, impinges on news organizations' principal commodity—that day's news. Thus my argument, in part, is this: Today's news is indeed biased—as it must inevitably be—and this bias can be best understood by understanding the concept, the conventions, and the ethic of objectivity.

Specifically, objectivity in journalism accounts for—or at least helps us understand—three principal developments in American journalism; each of these developments contributes to the bias or ideology of news. First, objective reporting is biased against what the press typically defines as its role in a democracy—that of a Fourth Estate, the watchdog role, an adversary press. Indeed, objectivity in journalism is biased in favor of the status quo; it is inherently conservative to the extent that it encourages reporters to rely on what sociologist Alvin Gouldner so appropriately describes as the "managers of the status quo'—the prominent and the élite. Second, objective reporting is biased against independent thinking; it emasculates the intellect by treating it as a disinterested spectator. Finally, objective reporting is biased against the very idea of responsibility; the day's news is viewed as something journalists are compelled to report, not something they are responsible for creating.

This last point, I think, is most important. Despite a renewed interest in professional ethics, the discussion continues to evade questions of morality and responsibility. Of course, this doesn't mean that journalists are immoral. Rather, it means that journalists today are largely amoral. Objectivity in journalism effectively erodes the very foundation on which rests a responsible press. . . .

Objectivity as an Ideal

As early as 1924 objectivity appeared as an ethic, an ideal subordinate only to truth itself. In his study of the *Ethics of Journalism*, Nelson Crawford devoted three full chapters to the principles of objectivity. Thirty years later, in 1954, Louis Lyons, then curator for the Nieman Fellowship program at Harvard, was describing objectivity as a "rock-bottom" imperative. Apparently unfazed by Wisconsin's Senator Joseph McCarthy, Lyons portrayed objectivity as the ultimate discipline of journalism. "It is at the bottom of all sound reporting—indispensable as the core of the writer's capacity." More recently, in 1973, the Society of Professional Journalists, Sigma Delta Chi formally enshrined the idea of objectivity when it adopted as part of its Code of Ethics a paragraph characterizing objective reporting as an attainable goal and a standard of performance toward which journalists should strive. "We honor those who achieve it," the Society proclaimed.

Legitimized by the Courts

So well ingrained are the principles of objective reporting that the judiciary is beginning to acknowledge them. In a 1977 federal appellate decision, *Edwards v. National Audubon Society,* a case described by media attorney Floyd Abrams as a landmark decision in that it may prove to be the next evolutionary stage in the development of the public law of libel, a new and novel privilege emerged. It was the first time the courts explicitly recognized objective reporting as a standard of journalism worthy of First Amendment protection.

Unexamined Assumptions

The complaint that we [journals of opinion] are shrill, captious or carping can, of course, be a euphemism for the fact that journals of critical opinion are critical—that most of them have rejected the myth of objectivity (also called fairness, but it amounts to the same thing) that pervades the mass media. The media still purports to separate facts from values and opinions, ghetto-izing the latter on editorial and Op-Ed pages. Interpretation is often banished to a no man's land, labeled News Analysis so as not to be mistaken for the real stuff. . . .

Of course, even publications in the (shifting) center operate on political premises; it is simply that their assumptions remain unexamined. In that way, the conventions of ostensibly objective reporting reinforce the status quo. Credibility these days is conferred largely by a moderation of tone, the appearance of evenhandedness. Independent magazines—left *and* right—exist to violate this conspiracy of coolness, the false equation, which has become today's dogma, between moderate and credible.

Victor Navasky, *The Nation,* June 8, 1985.

In what appeared to be an inconsequential story published in *The New York Times* in 1972—on page 33—five scientists were accused of being paid liars, men paid by the pesticide industry to lie about the use of DDT and its effect on bird life. True to the form of objective reporting, the accusation was fully attributed—to a fully identified official of the National Audubon Society. The scientists, of course, were given an opportunity to deny the accusation. Only one of the scientists, however, was quoted by name and he described the accusation as "almost libelous." What was newsworthy about the story, obviously, was the accusation; and with the exception of one short paragraph, the reporter more or less provided a forum for the National Audubon Society.

No Actual Malice

Three of the five scientists filed suit. While denying punitive damages, a jury awarded compensatory damages against the *Times* and one of the Society's officials. The *Times*, in turn, asked a federal District Court to overturn the verdict. The *Times* argued that the "actual malice" standard had not been met; since the scientists were "public figures," they were required to show that the *Times* knowingly published a falsehood or there was, on the part of the *Times*, a reckless disregard for whether the accusation was true or false. The evidence before the court clearly indicated the latter—there was indeed a reckless disregard for whether the accusation was true or false. The reporter made virtually no effort to confirm the validity of the National Audubon Society's accusations. Also the story wasn't the kind of "hot news" (a technical term used by the courts) that required immediate dissemination; in fact ten days before the story was published the *Times* learned that two of the five scientists were not employed by the pesticide industry and thus could not have been "paid liars."

The *Times* appealed to the Second Circuit Court of Appeals, where the lower court's decision was overturned. In reversing the District Court, the Court of Appeals created a new First Amendment right, a new Constitutional defense in libel law—the privilege of "neutral reportage." "We do not believe," the Court of Appeals ruled, "that the press may be required to suppress newsworthy statements merely because it has serious doubts regarding their truth." The First Amendment, the Court said, "protects the accurate and disinterested reporting" of newsworthy accusations "regardless of the reporter's private views regarding their validity."

Objectivity vs. Responsibility

I mention the details of the *Edwards* case only because it illustrates so well the consequences of the ethic of objectivity. First, it illustrates a very basic tension between objectivity and responsibility. Objective reporting virtually precludes responsible reporting, if by responsible reporting we mean a willingness on the part of the reporter to be accountable for what is reported. Objectivity requires only that reporters be accountable for *how* they report, not what they report. The *Edwards* Court made this very clear: "The public interest in being fully informed," the Court said, demands that the press be afforded the freedom to report newsworthy accusations "without assuming responsibility for them."

Second, the *Edwards* case illustrates the unfortunate bias of objective reporting—a bias in favor of leaders and officials, the prominent and the élite. It is an unfortunate bias because it runs counter to the important democratic assumption that statements made by ordinary citizens are as valuable as statements made by the prominent and the élite. In a democracy, public debate depends on separating individuals from their powers and privileges in the larger society; otherwise debate itself becomes a source of domination. But *Edwards* reinforces prominence as a news value; it reinforces the use of official sources, official records, official channels. Tom Wicker underscored the bias of the *Edwards* case when he observed recently that "objective journalism almost always favors Establishment positions and exists not least to avoid offense to them."

Journalists Denied Citizenship

Objectivity also has unfortunate consequences for the reporter, the individual journalist. Objective reporting has stripped reporters of their creativity and their imagination; it has robbed journalists of their passion and their perspective. Objective reporting has transformed journalism into something more technical than intellectual; it has turned the art of story-telling into the technique of report writing. And most unfortunate of all, objective reporting has denied journalists their citizenship; as disinterested observers, as impartial reporters, journalists are expected to be morally disengaged and politically inactive.

Covert Prejudice

At bottom, I believe objectivity is a figleaf for covert prejudice. The point is not to equate objectivity with truth. It was objective to quote Joe McCarthy during the 1950's; it was the truth to report that most of what he had to say was unfounded slander. . . .

The goal for all journalists should be to come as close to complex truth as humanly possible. But the truth does not always reside exactly in the middle. Truth is not the square root of two balanced quotes. I don't believe I should be "objective" about racism, or the tax loopholes for the rich. . . . Certain facts are not morally neutral.

Jack Newfield, *Liberating the Media*, 1974.

Journalists have become—to borrow James Carey's terminology—"professional communicators," a relatively passive link between sources and audiences. With neither the need nor the opportunity to develop a critical perspective from which to assess the events, the issues, and the personalities he or she is assigned to cover, the objective reporter tends to function as a translator—translating the specialized language of sources into a language intelligible to a lay audience.

In his frequently cited study of Washington correspondents—a study published nearly fifty years ago—Leo Rosten found that a "pronounced majority" of the journalists he interviewed considered themselves inadequate to cope with the bewildering complexities of our nation's policies and politics. As Rosten described it, the Washington press corps was a frustrated and exasperated group of prominent journalists more or less resigned to their role as mediators, translators. "To do the job," one reporter told Rosten, "what you know or understand isn't important. You've got to know whom to ask." Even if you don't understand what's being said, Rosten was told, you just take careful notes and write it up verbatim: "Let my readers figure it out. I'm their reporter, not their teacher."

That was fifty years ago. Today, the story is pretty much the same. Two years ago another study of Washington correspondents was published, a book by Stephen Hess called *The Washington Reporters*. For the most part, Hess found, stories coming out of Washington were little more than a "mosaic of facts and quotations from sources" who were participants in an event or who had knowledge of the event. Incredibly, Hess found that for nearly three-quarters of the stories he studied, reporters relied on no documents—only interviews. And when reporters did use documents, those documents were typically press clippings—stories they had written or stories written by their colleagues.

And so what does objectivity mean? It means that sources supply the sense and substance of the day's news. Sources provide the arguments, the rebuttals, the explanations, the criticism. Sources put forth the ideas while other sources challenge those ideas. Journalists, in their role as professional communicators, merely provide a vehicle for these exchanges. . . .

Naively Empirical View

No doubt the press has responded to many of the more serious consequences of objective reporting. But what is significant is that the response has been to amend the conventions of objectivity, not to abandon them. The press has merely refined the canons of objective reporting; it has not dislodged them.

What remains fundamentally unchanged is the journalist's naively empirical view of the world, a belief in the separation of facts and values, a belief in the existence of *a* reality—the reality of empirical facts. Nowhere is this belief more evident than when news is defined as something external to—and independent of— the journalist. The very vocabulary used by journalists when they talk about news underscores their belief that news is "out there," presumably waiting to be *exposed* or *uncovered* or at least *gathered*.

This is the essence of objectivity, and this is precisely why it is so very difficult for journalism to consider questions of ethics and morality. Since news exists "out there"—apparently independent of the reporter—journalists can't be held responsible for it. And since they are not responsible for the news being there, how can we expect journalists to be accountable for the consequences of merely reporting it?

What objectivity has brought about, in short, is a disregard for the consequences of newsmaking. A few years ago Walter Cronkite offered this interpretation of journalism: "I don't think it is any of our business what the moral, political, social, or economic effect of our reporting is. I say let's go with the job of reporting— and let the chips fall where they may."

Contrast that to John Dewey's advice: that "our chief moral business is to become acquainted with consequences."

News Is Their Creation

I am inclined to side with Dewey. Only to the extent that journalists are held accountable for the consequences of their actions can there be said to be a responsible press. But we are not going to be able to hold journalists accountable for the consequences of their actions until they acknowledge that news is their creation, a creation for which they are fully responsible. And we are not going to have much success convincing journalists that news is created, not reported, until we can successfully challenge the conventions of objectivity.

The task, then, is to liberate journalism from the burden of objectivity by demonstrating—as convincingly as we can—that objective reporting is more of a custom than a principle, more a habit of mind than a standard of performance. And by showing that objectivity is largely a matter of efficiency—efficiency that serves, as far as I can tell, only the needs and interests of the owners of the press, not the needs and interests of talented writers and certainly not the needs and interests of the larger society.

31

"U.S. journalism is not the proudly independent institution it believes itself to be, but instead defers to the . . . established perspectives of the national security state."

The Media Are Biased in Favor of the Government

William A. Dorman

Government officials often complain that the media are hostile to them and interfere in the carrying out of government policy. But in the following viewpoint, William A. Dorman insists that in reporting foreign affairs, the media are actually too supportive of Washington's goals. Dorman, a professor of journalism at California State University in Sacramento, states that the media are dependent on government officials for much of their information and share many of the government's assumptions about foreign affairs.

As you read, consider the following questions:

1. What kinds of ideological assumptions does Dorman think the media share with government policy makers?
2. Why, according to Dorman, does the denial of bias on the part of members of the media actually make them more susceptible to bias?
3. What suggestions does the author make about how the media can free themselves from bias?

William A. Dorman, "Peripheral Vision: U.S. Journalism and the Third World," *World Policy Journal,* Summer 1986. Reprinted with permission.

U.S. journalism is not the proudly independent institution it believes itself to be, but instead defers all to often to the established perspectives and formulations of the national security state. This virtually precludes any possibility of a serious debate on the conventional premises of U.S. foreign policy.

This failure of journalism to exert an effective reality check on policymakers—to provide a means of gauging whether policy is based on evidence and concrete facts or on self-delusions and misperceptions—has particularly serious consequences for U.S. understanding of the Third World.

Distorting Reality

Clearly, . . . all developing countries are not given equal treatment. U.S. public opinion is far more negative toward the Sandinistas than it ever was toward the Shah [of Iran]; Americans have heard a great deal more about the agony of Afghanistan than they have about the suffering of East Timor; Allende [of Chile] was subjected to close and constant scrutiny, while the problems that fester under Pinochet's dictatorship are the subject of only occasional, mild concern. . . .

Indeed, coverage of the Third World is highly unlikely to improve until the press comes to grips with *subjective* factors that impinge on the journalistic process. Yet American journalists strongly believe that the U.S. press is beyond ideology—that the news media are autonomous, models of civic truth-seeking, serious auditors of the state—because of a number of professional rules and practices that, if routinely followed, supposedly ensure non-biased coverage of events. Ironically, these conventions can actually serve to perpetuate the ideology and ethnocentrism that distort reporting from the Third World.

False Objectivity

Take, for example, the prevailing assumption that objectivity is best achieved when the correspondent uses only direct or indirect quotations from all *authoritative* sides of an issue, letting assertions of fact stand on their own without interpretation or comment. The reporter is not supposed to interject his or her own opinion, substantiated or not; statements of opinion can only come from others. Background material can be used, of course, but it must come from *established* authority.

This practice operates on the time-honored American principle that if there are two diametrically opposed claims to truth, the truth must lie somewhere between. Unfortunately, such a principle overlooks the possibility that one or both claimants are lying, misinformed, fantasizing, or, more likely, slanting their statements toward the particular conclusions they want their audiences to reach. History has a clear lesson to add to that possibility: the greater the threat that the truth poses to established authority, the less trustworthy are that authority's claims to truth. Only a reporter's personal judgment, based on systematic knowledge of the issue at hand, could make the fine discriminations needed to assess the validity of statements by established, official sources. But journalistic practice routinely excludes such assessments from news stories—overlooking what should have been learned from the Joseph McCarthy and Watergate periods.

Media Adopt Official Views

What is amazing in this country is the speed and the enthusiasm with which the national media adopt official values and promote the consensus almost before it is put forth by the authorities. Whether the issue is terrorism, drugs, the Statue of Liberty, Nicaragua, Libya or the Philippines, there is an urgent imperative to spout the line. It is almost impossible to find significant, principled dissent in the mainstream press and on the networks at anywhere near the quality and quantity that was common during the time of the Vietnam War and Watergate.

Perhaps the paranoid projects of AIM [Accuracy in Media] and the other right-wing neoconservative lobbies have eroded the tradition of independent reportage. Perhaps the rewards for conformity are too great to turn down, or the support system for dissent too weak to offer an alternative to the institutions that engineer consent.

The Nation, September 13, 1986.

Furthermore, journalists are taught to ignore a reality that courtroom lawyers forget at their peril: how you use the facts, what interpretation you make of demonstrable truth, is as important as the facts themselves. A lawyer building his case is conscious of the importance of emphasis, shading, and nuance in producing a cumulative effect that makes some facts stand out to a jury and others fade. Yet journalists have allowed rules of objectivity to stand in for their own thoughtful analysis or informed assessment of official statements. In the process, those statements are given undue weight; officials are given chance after chance to sway the jury of public opinion to their way of thinking. . . .

Officials as News Sources

Perhaps of even greater concern than these trends, though, is the extent to which Washington officials not only provide interpretation but also serve as sources for news about the Third World. Most foreign news reaches the mainstream press through routine channels that are hardly disinterested and are likely, in fact, to be officials or agencies of the U.S. government. All too frequently, these sources are allowed to remain anonymous.

This reliance on U.S. officials—and, often, their Third World client counterparts—makes the news media part of the closed information loop. The public frequently hears an echo of official assumption rather than a fresh and critical voice. . . .

The Power To Define

Media deference to Washington's favored sources also means that the labels, stereotypes, and characterizations applied to events and personalities in the Third World tend to be handed down by the administration rather than formulated by journalists. The terms and boundaries of discourse are thus defined by elites— not by the events the discourse purports to be about. Harried correspondents working in the field or in Washington are prone to find the White House's authoritative, prefabricated prose familiar, convenient, and safe. Such facile labeling, however, tends to radically oversimplify complex economic, social, and political realities in the Third World, and furthermore to cast the geopolitical drama with Washington's choice of heroes and villains. As observers from Lewis Carroll to George Orwell have warned, in politics the power to define is everything. . . .

Generally, such expressions as "left-wing," "communist," "Marxist," and "Soviet-supported" appear regularly without justification or explanation. These pejorative phrases act as buzz-words: they are short, they have high emotional content, and they are widely accepted as having an understood meaning. In popular discourse, Washington's critics have few equivalent buzzwords to argue for a contrary position; and even when they do have such words—"dictator" is one example—the press is often reluctant to use them.

Thus the foreign policy establishment clearly has the upper hand in setting the meanings of words and symbols and labels. As a result, the administration's vision often comes to be received opinion, reinforcing White House policy, while critics struggle simply to be heard. . . .

Denial of Ideology

These largely external factors are not, however, the only constraints on media coverage of the Third World. Despite American journalism's image of itself as impartial, and despite (in fact, partly *because* of) journalistic practices meant to eliminate subjective bias, the U.S. press is in fact severely hampered by its own ideology. This may be less of a problem in how the national press covers the narrow realm of domestic bipartisan electoral politics, where contemporary journalism has evolved an elaborate system of checks and balances to keep *personal* bias out of reporting. But no such arrangements exist to safeguard against the effects of ideology—shared or collective bias—in reporting on the Third World. These biases become more difficult to detect, and hence more insidious, the more broadly they are shared. . . .

It is at the level of internalized restraints that ideology operates most effectively. Ideology, as used here, simply means a well-ordered worldview—a generalized political consciousness, a kind of political white noise. This consciousness, or subconsciousness, consists of broad assumptions about America's place in the world vis-á-vis other nations, and typically includes certain prejudices and biases about Third World peoples. This is not to say that a journalist necessarily holds a set of doctrinaire, highly systematic, rigidly imposed categories that cause him to shape his writing toward a particular political end, but that he has a particular, characteristic *perspective* that subtly affects all of his work. Take the example of the reporter who recalled covering Chile under Allende: "I didn't 'interpret' the Allende regime as [being] against the best interests of the U.S. government. I *knew* it."

Eager Allies

Common class interests often make for common political perspectives. When it comes to "meeting the challenge of Communism," for instance, media owners are eager allies rather than independent critics of the nation's political leaders, sharing the same view about the desirability of the existing economic system at home and abroad and the pernicious nature of those who might want to change it through agitation and class struggle.

Michael Parenti, *Inventing Reality*, 1986.

These types of widely shared ideological assumptions—about the threat posed by the Soviet Union, about the nature of politics, economic development, and rebellion in the Third World—have caused the news media in many cases to follow the cues of official Washington rather than exercising independent journalistic judgment. The press has completely accepted the dominant paradigm of an East-West struggle. Developing countries are perceived and portrayed merely as the stakes in a zero-sum game between Washington and Moscow. Journalists reflexively accept the need to contain the Soviet Union and allocate news time and space accordingly, creating a badly distorted news map for the public.

Ideology also has much to do with setting the news agenda, with determining what qualifies as news. The result for the Third World is a pronounced double standard. The economic failures, human rights violations, and abusive treatment of minorities on the part of those Third World countries that oppose U.S. interests are treated as newsworthy, while similar behavior in client regimes goes relatively ignored (at least until the client is in the process of being deposed—Marcos, for example). . . .

Equally troubling, policymakers' strategic assumptions are largely left unexamined and unchallenged; only tactics come in for a critical view. This tendency reflects a general deference to the national security state, which is as much a worldview as a set of institutions. The whole news-gathering system in America is structured in a way that favors the national security state as traditionally defined. . . .

In fact, it is precisely because journalists believe they are above and beyond ideology that they are most susceptible to its effects. Journalists have been trained to think that by scrupulously following the narrow rules of objectivity they will remain free of ideology's clutches. They are encouraged to believe in a state of innocence that simply does not exist and certainly cannot be achieved under the rules they follow. This belief prevents mainstream journalists from moving toward an authentic form of objectivity, which involves, first, recognizing one's own biases. The effects of such bias can be dealt with and at least minimized, but only if journalists recognize the problem and if reportorial conventions are changed to compensate for it. . . .

A Civil Voice

What the American press has largely lost, and needs to recover, is a journalistic "civil voice"—one with "proud recourse to moral authority, dependence on unmediated expression, respect for individual opinion and independent judgment."

For such a voice to emerge, journalists would have to come to grips with the deep-seated subjective factors that underlie their own ideological biases. Everything in mainstream journalism works against this, however. Thus it may be necessary to approach the problem from without, by focusing attention on the need for change in professional practice. The conventions of journalism, especially as they apply to defense issues and the Third World, need to be thoroughly reexamined.

As a first step to restoring journalism's civil voice, the press might work to *anticipate* major policy debates and Third World crises rather than waiting for revolutions to occur or for the White House to set the agenda. . . .

In this connection, the press must begin to actively seek information sources outside the charmed circle of Washington policymakers, bureaucrats, and the defense intellectuals who serve as the pilot fish for Cold War policy. This means that journalists must widen their definition of quotable authorities to include those who question Washington's goals, not just its tactics. And those goals need to be criticized in news columns and broadcasts as well as on op-ed pages. Furthermore, the press must seek out dissenting views in client states as enthusiastically as it does in those countries deemed hostile to U.S. interests.

Yet another practice that must be either abandoned or radically changed is the use of unnamed Washington sources. This custom has come to serve only the interests of policymakers: whatever journalists say about the value of deep backgrounding, the record shows otherwise. How many times must the media be lied to, duped, or manipulated before this simple fact sinks in? There is no reason why journalists covering the Third World cannot emphasize documentary evidence, which is almost always attributable, rather than working the phones and depending on interviews. . . .

These are only first steps toward recapturing the civil voice that American journalism must have in order to serve as a watchdog on U.S. policy.

"Many in the media are super critical of our leaders, while foreign countries—including our worst enemies—often get surprisingly gentle treatment."

The Media Are Biased Against the Government

Michael Ledeen

William Dorman, the author of the opposing article, argues that the media are too supportive of the goals of the American government concerning foreign policy. But in the following viewpoint Michael Ledeen, a senior fellow at the Center for Strategic and International Studies at Georgetown University, insists that the media's portrayal of foreign affairs reveals a bias against the US government.

As you read, consider the following questions:

1. Why do journalists rely on embassy officials for information on foreign affairs, according to the author?
2. According to Ledeen, what is the double standard used by the media in reporting foreign affairs?
3. Ledeen argues that the media's use of leaks from unnamed government sources harms government policymakers. By contrast, William Dorman, author of the previous viewpoint, sees the use of leaks by officials as a method of manipulating the media to support government policy. Who do you think is correct? Why?

Michael Ledeen, "The Press and Foreign Policy," *Public Opinion*, August/September 1984, pp. 5-7, 60. Reprinted with permission of American Enterprise Institute.

Like the other members of our policy elite, the leaders of the Fourth Estate suffer from both ignorance of the world and from the abstract moralism that permeates our popular culture. But writers and broadcasters are rarely held accountable for their mistakes; politicians, diplomats, and even professors may pay for their errors with their political lives and professional careers. And while some academics and diplomats have career interests in learning about countries and cultures other than our own, the media figures have every reason to concentrate on a narrowly American context. Careers depend upon "making air" in the United States and upon being published prominently in American newspapers and magazines. The best place for an ambitious media personality is New York or Washington, while an overseas assignment is often an unpleasant detour on the career path.

Media Ignorance, Apathy

It is difficult to learn the ins and outs of any society, and especially in a foreign country and culture. With career inducements pointing back toward Washington and New York, rare indeed is the foreign correspondent who develops real foreign sources or gains deep insight into another country. The news from abroad thus remains locked in an American context.

Foreign news, then, will almost always have an American angle to it, because the correspondent wants to attract American attention, and because his superiors—the editors, news directors, and producers who control so much of the television and print news— need to keep their ratings up. This is difficult, since Americans aren't much interested in foreign news except as it affects them directly and dramatically. Consequently, our media look for scandals involving the American government, or some similar drama with a hometown hook. And here, the natural ally of the journalist is the American embassy official. The alliance is often very productive, for it serves the needs of both. First, such officials relieve the journalist of the need to learn a foreign language, master a foreign political culture, or evaluate the reliability of foreign sources. Second, like the journalists, our embassy officials are looking for the American angles. Third, the diplomat and the journalist may have a common interest in hyping a story. In fairness to our correspondents abroad, it should be noted that most foreign government officials are reluctant to talk candidly with American news people; if they have something important to say or leak, they will usually work with their own national press. . . .

Only One Side Investigated

Many in the media are super critical of our leaders, while foreign countries—including our worst enemies—often get surprisingly gentle treatment. Investigative journalism is rarely unleashed on other countries, but when it is, the other countries are typically friends and/or allies of ours. The most obvious examples are Israel, the Shah's Iran, El Salvador, and Chile. Why this unfair treatment?

In part, the imbalance in investigative zeal can be explained on purely operational grounds: our totalitarian opponents do not open their archives to journalists, nor do they leak as much as do officials in the United States and other democratic countries or inefficient dictatorships. In the Warsaw Pact, leakers are treated as traitors; in America, they are often lionized. And, of course, there is no Freedom of Information Act in the Soviet empire. Yet, whatever the differences in obtaining information, it is evident that the elite media have developed a double standard for reporting the news.

The President's Censors

When President Reagan visited China he made several broadcasts for use over the Chinese television. Some parts of his message were deleted before it was shown. Chris Wallace, one of the young network reporters who accompanied the President, asked him how he liked having his material censored.

"It didn't bother me a bit," Reagan replied. "You people do it all the time."

Richard A. Snyder, *Vital Speeches of the Day*, January 1, 1985.

The United States and its allies are held up against standards that are not applied to the Soviet Union and its satellites and proxies. Relatively minor human rights transgressions in friendly countries (especially those ruled by authoritarian governments of the Right) are given far more attention, and are subjected to more intense criticism, than are far graver sins of countries hostile to us. Accusations against our enemies are often treated more skeptically than those directed against us, even though our government, along with those of most other democracies, strains mightily to tell the truth. The Soviets, along with other totalitarian regimes, have entire governmental agencies to spread systematic distortions of the truth (the most celebrated example is the KGB's Disinformation Directorate). . . .

To be sure, there are some distinguished American correspondents who produce some superb reportage, but it is impossible to get an accurate picture of the world from the American press. And even when the real story is written, it is often years late, as in the case of China. During the Maoist regime, one rarely heard about the horrors of the Cultural Revolution, but once a moderate liberalization had set in, our media began to tell the real story that they had spiked for years.

41

Stories that appear late have far less effect than those that come out as "hot news," just as small corrections that are published or announced a few days after a damaging headline do little to establish the truth in the minds of readers and viewers.

Media Favor Our Enemies

It is difficult to escape the conclusion that much of this writing and broadcasting rests upon political conviction rather than operational difficulties. In the case of the plot to kill the Pope, we would have been deluged with stories had there been the slightest indication that the American government was involved (and I know at least one top television correspondent who spent weeks traveling around the world trying to prove just that). . . .

The pattern is to be found in almost every area of international news, with the result that our readers and viewers are rarely reminded that there is a great difference between ourselves and our principal adversaries. If the West prevails in a conflict, we will strain to support democratic forces and a peaceful evolution toward a more equitable system. If the Soviet Union prevails, the totalitarian curtain falls over the victims. Yet a surprising number of journalists treat Soviet actions as morally neutral—or even vaguely humanitarian—and our reaction against them as automatic, predictable anticommunism.

The Use of Leaks

The media's suspicion of our government, combined with their limited understanding of the world at large, has a devastating effect upon our foreign policy. Suspicious as they are of American intentions, and bolstered by court rulings that seem to give the press license to seek out and publish any and all governmental secrets, the media damage our ability to design and conduct good policy in ways they rarely imagine.

The leak, through which sensitive information flows from the government to the press, is detrimental to policy primarily because it makes serious discussion almost impossible. People, whether our own government officials or the leaders of foreign countries, are unwilling to speak their minds if anything they say may appear in print. If leaks become endemic, our own policy discussions will be restricted to a handful of people who trust each other, thus limiting the richness and variety of ideas that are brought forward through the system. And along with the limiting of ideas, we have less reliable information to think about. Leaders often say one thing in public and something quite different in private conversation, and while Americans may consider this immoral, it has been a legitimate form of political behavior for centuries and will not be changed by American press exposés. It is vitally important for the leaders of the United States to know the real state of affairs, and this can occur only if foreign leaders feel free

Bill Garner for *The Washington Times*. Reprinted with permission.

to speak their minds to our diplomats. But they do not like to see their private thoughts in the newspapers, and they will not share their real beliefs (let alone their secrets) unless they are certain that confidences will be respected. . . .

While leaks are generally defended by media officials on the grounds of the public's "right to know," in reality they are part of the Washington political power game, as well as part of the policy process. The leaker may be currying favor with the media, or may be planting information to influence policy. In the first case, he is helping himself by enhancing the prestige of a journalist; in the second, he is using the media as a stage for his preferred policies. In either instance, it closes the circle: the leak begins with a political motive, is advanced by a politicized media, and continues because of politics. Although some of the journalists think *they* are doing the work, they are more often than not instruments of the process, not prime movers.

Until recently, it looked as if the media had convinced the public that journalists were more reliable than the government; thus, many citizens came to believe that the media were the *best* sources of information. When the media challenged a governmental official, the public's presumption was that the official was wrong. This may be changing. With the passage of time, the media have lost luster. They—having grown large and powerful—receive the same public skepticism other large institutions in the society do. A series of media scandals has contributed. The Westmoreland v. Columbia Broadcasting System trial—and all of the publicity it will receive—may tarnish the image further. The public's lack of outrage at the exclusion of journalists from Grenada may have contributed, too. For these reasons, many Americans have concluded that the media are no more credible than the government is, and public opinion surveys reflect much ambivalence about the press. . . .

Media Must Be Accountable

The media must be held accountable for their activities, just like every other significant institution in our society, and the media must be made to earn the public's trust, not granted power over a government afraid to fight in the public arena. We badly need media that give the public—and the government—a thorough, dispassionate picture of the world at large. That can happen only if media errors are exposed, if successful careers can be made outside New York and Washington, and if the relationship between policy makers and correspondents is rendered more responsible: leaks of sensitive material and publication of irresponsible stories must cease.

"That there is a diversity of trivial publications does not mean there is a diversity of ideas, ideologies, and political information."

The Media Are Hampered by Special Interests

Michael Parenti

There are those who point to the ownership of the television networks, major newspapers, and wire services by major corporations as proof that the major news media are actually conservative supporters of the status quo. Michael Parenti is an activist and author of several books on the media. He argues in the following viewpoint that this corporate control expresses itself in an increased centralizing of information sources and in the proliferation of recreational publications meant to lull the public into complacency.

As you read, consider the following questions:

1. Why, according to Parenti, is the appearance of diversity in commercial publications misleading?
2. To Parenti, what is a more accurate description of the American media than a "free market of ideas"?
3. Parenti believes that the media can still be influenced by those outside the corporate world. How? Do you agree or disagree?

Michael Parenti, "Does the U.S. Have a Free Press?" *The Witness*, March 1985. Reprinted with permission.

It is commonly believed that the United States is a society endowed with "a free and independent press," but the reality is something else. Who specifically owns the mass media in the United States?

Who Controls the Media?

Ten huge business and financial corporations control the three major television and radio networks, 34 subsidiary television stations, 201 cable television systems, 62 radio stations, 20 record companies, 59 magazines including *Time* and *Newsweek*, 58 newspapers including the *New York Times*, the *Washington Post*, the *Wall Street Journal* and the *Los Angeles Times*, 41 book publishers, and various motion picture companies like Columbia Pictures and Twentieth-Century Fox. Three quarters of the major stockholders of the three broadcast networks are banks such as Chase Manhattan, Morgan Guaranty Trust, and Bank of America. These banks, in turn, are controlled mostly by four economic empires: the Mellons, the Morgans, the Rockefellers, and the DuPonts—the same family groups that dominate the financial, mining, manufacturing, agricultural, and oil industries of the United States and much of the world.

The overall pattern with regard to the U.S. news media is one of increasing concentration of ownership and earnings. According to a 1982 survey, independent newspapers are being gobbled up by the big newspaper companies at the rate of 50 or 60 a year. Ten newspaper corporations earn over half of all newspaper revenues in the United States. The giant newspaper companies buy up not only independent papers but other giant companies that might control dozens of newspapers themselves. In 1978, Gannett Corporation, one of the biggest, described itself as "a nation-wide newspaper company with 78 dailies in 30 states."

Less than 4% of American cities have competing newspapers under separate ownership; and in cities where there is a "choice," the papers offer little variety in editorial policy, being mostly politically conservative. Most of the "independent" newspapers rely on the wire services and larger newspapers for syndicated columnists and for national and international news. Like local television and radio stations, they are not really independent but quite dependent on the big news producers.

A Profitable Business

As with any business, the mass media's first obligation is to make money for their owners. Although declining in numbers, newspapers continue to be a major U.S. profit-making business, employing over 432,000 people. Through mergers, staff cutting, and reliance on central news service, the large conglomerates show handsome profits. In 1980, for instance, the annual advertising revenues of newspapers in the United States was $15.6 billion, with many billions more going to radio and television. A typical medium-circulation newspaper makes a 23% profit each year. The American press can hardly pretend to be a critic of giant U.S. corporations and exorbitant business profits, since the press enjoys profits that equal those of most oil companies.

Break Up Oligopoly

The reason that the media are so easy for a few powerful institutions to control and dominate is that few people bother to consider the problems posed by minimal restrictions on the ownership of communications media by private capital. There is no restriction on the ownership of print media, and there is an effort, led by the churches and the radical right, to remove the ownership restrictions on broadcast media. (Currently six television and six radio stations are the maximums, and no two may be in the same market.) The only way to break up a monopoly or oligopoly is for laws to be passed which make them illegal. In the case of the media, it will be necessary to restrict the ownership of newspapers and other print media in a manner similar to that of television and radio.

Brian Lynch, *American Atheist*, December 1986.

Most newspapers, magazines, radio and TV networks, and movie studios in the United States are themselves giant corporations or subsidiaries of larger corporate conglomerates. Consider *Time* magazine—whose editors, according to one ex-*Time* reporter, "have never been shy about its incestuous relations with the captains of industry." *Time,* along with five or six other national publications, is owned by Time Inc., a colossal multinational company with yearly revenues of $2.5 billion. Time Inc. also owns several large publishing firms in the United States and has investments in others in Germany, France, Mexico and Japan. In addition, Time Inc. owns lumber and paper industries and is one of the biggest landowners in the United States. It also owns a marketing data company, a furniture manufacturer, several real estate and land development ventures, a group of Chicago suburban newspapers, American Television and Communications Corporation, and other television interests. . . .

While having an abundance of numbers and giving the appearance of great diversity, the U.S. news media actually offer a remarkably homogenized fare. News services for dailies throughout the entire nation are provided by the Associated Press (AP), United Press International (UPI), the *New York Times* news service, the *Los-Angeles Times-Washington Post* news service, and several foreign news services like Reuters. The ideological viewpoint of these news conduits are much the same, standardized and narrow in the kind of information they allow the American public to receive. The same conservative commentators, along with an occasional liberal one, appear in newspapers coast to coast on the same day.

Many newspapers in the smaller cities publish editorials and political cartoons supplied by the central news services, and other features that specialize in blandness and in the implicit acceptance of the existing system and existing social conditions. The blandness disappears, however, when law and order, communism, the Soviet "threat," labor strikes, and minority unrest are discussed.

More and more newspaper space is given over to "soft" rather than "hard" news, to trivialized features and gossip items, to stories about movie and television stars, to crime, scandal, and sensationalism. Television, radio, and newspaper coverage of national and local affairs is usually scant, superficial, and oriented toward "events" and "personalities," consisting of a few short "headline stories" and a number of conservative or simply banal commentaries and editorials.

Uniform News

Pouring into editorial offices and news rooms across the United States from the centralized news-service syndicates are photographs, news features, women's features, comic strips, sports columns, advice to the lovelorn, horoscopes, book reviews, and film and theater reviews. Whichever newspaper one reads or television station one views, in whatever part of the United States, one is struck by the indistinguishable and immediately familiar quality of the news and political views presented and of the people presenting them. One confronts a precooked, controlled, centralized, national news industry that is in sharp contrast to the "pluralistic diversity" of opinion and information which is supposed to prevail in the United States.

Americans are taught that they live in a society that has a free market of ideas where information, images, and viewpoints circulate freely. But the notion of a free market is a misleading metaphor. A "market" suggests a place of plentitude, choice, and variety, with the consumer moving from stall to stall as at any bazaar, sampling and picking from an array of wares. The existing news media market of ideas is more like the larger economic market of which it is a part: oligopolistic, standardized, and most accessible to those who possess vast amounts of capital, or who hold views that are pleasing to the possessors of capital.

To be sure, there is a vast array of magazines and other publications in the United States, magazines for motorcycle owners, for brides, for fishing, hunting, and outdoor life, for home furnishing, for people who want to lose weight, for people who want to lift weights, for music fans, movie fans, and sports fans. Relatively few of these have anything to do with meaningful political and social affairs; most are devoted to the distractions of mass media entertainment and consumerism. That there is a diversity of trivial publications does not mean there is a diversity of ideas, ideologies, and political information.

No Diversity

One need only to look as far as Europe to see the problems with the American press. Compared to the vibrant and diverse political perspectives available in European news, their American counterparts are embarrassingly homogeneous. Political variations in the three U.S. networks' broadcasts may only be detectable in measurements of parts per billion. Each sits astride the same political fence, frightened to lean to either side in order to not offend viewers—or more importantly, to not offend sponsors. Opinions which stray too far on either side are routinely excluded from the 22 minutes of network news offered each evening, stripping both passion and diversity from the U.S. political debate.

Peter Dykstra, *Greenpeace*, January/March 1987.

None of the above is to be taken as an invitation to lose heart and lapse into discouragement and quietude. Making ourselves aware that the news media are not free and independent, not neutral and objective, is a necessary first step in defending ourselves from the media's ideational manipulation. What can we do?

An Available Alternative

First, seek out alternative media like progressive, listener-supported radio stations and publications like *The Witness, Sojourners,* the *Nation,* the *Guardian, Monthly Review,* the *Progressive,* the *Daily World, Political Affairs, CovertAction,* and others. Many religious, environmental, minority, student, peace, gay, and women's groups and labor unions have their own newsletters and newspapers which reach millions of people and often carry important articles on issues suppressed by the business-owned media. It has been the alternative media, and not the mainstream media, that first raised critical questions about environmental devastation, nuclear power, inequitable economic policies, the arms race, military spending, U.S. intervention in the Third World, repression of dissent at home, corporate class power, and the like.

As the alternate media and the democratic forces of this society have generated momentum around particular issues, the major media have had to respond—often reluctantly, insufficiently, and disingenuously—but respond they must. If the owners of most of our media could have their way, the press would concentrate on human interest stories, cheery announcements about economic recovery, and patriotic editorials about the need to keep America strong. But to maintain its credibility, the press must give some attention to the realities people experience; it must deal with questions like: Why are my taxes so high? Why is the river so polluted? Why must my son register for the draft? The media's need to deal with these things—however haphazardly and insufficiently—is what leads conservatives to complain that the press is infected with "liberal" biases.

Also, to maintain its credibility and its appearance as a neutral and objective institution, the press allows the public some limited access, in the form of letters-to-the-editor and guest columns, and on local broadcast media—guest commentaries and call-in shows. Even the letters that do not get published and the calls that are heard only by station managers have an impact—sometimes.

Summary

In sum, to create a more democratic climate of opinion in our country we must (1) alert ourselves to the way the media manipulates, evades, and packages the news; (2) support and strengthen alternative media with subscriptions and contributions, recognizing them as a crucial and liberating source of information and analysis; (3) talk back to the major media, exposing their biases and distortions whenever possible, taking advantage of what few outlets we have in them; (4) continue to struggle for social justice, creating a reality that influences the controlled image field in which the media operate. We do not have the luxury to feel discouraged. The democratic forces of our society have won victories in the past against tremendous odds, and we will win more in the future. Indeed, the future itself depends on it.

"In a society where points of view range from serious commentary about foreign affairs to proposals for more nude beaches, there is clearly a good deal of diversity."

The Media Are Not Hampered by Special Interests

Everette E. Dennis

Many media critics point with alarm to the increased centralization of ownership of general interest publications. But Everette E. Dennis, a journalism professor at the University of Oregon, insists that such concern is overstated. In addition, Dennis argues that the proliferation of special interest magazines and of cable television systems insures that we will have ample sources of information.

As you read, consider the following questions:

1. To what does Dennis attribute the fear of increased centralization of newspapers? Why does he think these fears are unfounded?
2. What evidence does the author admit points toward decreased variety in newspapers?

Reprinted with permission of Macmillan Publishing Company from *Basic Issues in Mass Communication: A Debate* by Everette E. Dennis and John C. Merrill. Copyright © 1984 by Macmillan Publishing Company.

The response is predictable. A newspaper dies and editorialists throughout the nation declare that "a voice is lost and we are poorer for it." The early 1980s were devastating years for large afternoon daily newspapers (called PMs) as the *Philadelphia Bulletin, Cleveland Press, Washington Star, Minneapolis Star, Des Moines Tribune,* and *Oregon Journal* either died or were merged into larger, healthier morning dailies. It was a blow for diversity, a blow for media pluralism. Or was it?

The purpose of this discussion is to move beyond the usual knee-jerk reaction to the condition of "our declining dailies" and to get a more substantive understanding of media pluralism. To do that we have to get some things straight.

Issues of Pluralism

Debating about media pluralism requires a close look at one of the most curious and complex concepts in the field of mass communication. It is a strange mixture of constitutional history, economic theory, sociology, and good old-fashioned moralizing. To begin with, few would doubt that one of the intentions of the press freedom clause of the First Amendment was to allow for diversity of information and opinion. This diversity was to protect citizens from governmental control of information and ideas. Today we can add to this concern the fear many critics have of the private sector, which owns our communication system and which has profit, not pluralism, as its primary motivating force. In addition to the component of diversity of information and opinion, media pluralism also involves the existence of different ethnic and cultural subgroups in the population. A central assumption here is that no single subgroup should dominate the others.

When reduced to its fundamental features, media pluralism usually means two things: diversity of ownership and diversity of content in the communications available to the public. The two are thought to be interrelated. At one level it would seem that the question of whether media pluralism is expanding or shrinking requires only a simple empirical response. Can't we simply count the number of media organizations in society, see who owns them, and have an answer? The answer is "No, not exactly," for the problem is more complex and difficult to sort out because the number of voices is only a part of the equation. It's what's in them that counts and there is no easy, universally accepted way to measure diversity of content. The problem is even more clouded because deep-seated values, prevailing prejudices, and excessive moralizing engulf the notion of media diversity and pluralism.

For these reasons media pluralism is rarely the subject of rational debate. Critics snarl, growl, and carp. They use economic forecasts and other quantitative data as they see fit. Some of them think newspapers and other media outlets are mainly public service organizations, rather than economic entities. To them chain owners and other media managers are self-serving and essentially evil individuals who would package and sell off our democratic values if they could, to make a profit. Indeed, former *New York Times* reporter Molly Ivins once picked up on this with a bit of black humor when she told a convention of newspaper owners, "I thought you people would be a bunch of egg-sucking child molesters."

Just when the issue of media pluralism emerged is not clear, but by the 1920s critics like Oswald Garrison Villard of *The Nation* were decrying the growing economic concentration of the newspaper industry. Chain ownership, Villard and others believed, had unfortunate social consequences and would lessen chances for the Miltonian ideal wherein truth and falsehood could grapple in the market place of ideas. The fewer the voices, the less variety of information and opinion.

No Monopoly

No matter how the media voices are counted, they are far from a monopoly. There are three national television networks, plus *ad hoc* networks. There are four national radio networks, plus innumerable interconnected stations. There is AP and UPI providing the nation's newspapers with reports, plus numerous Washington newspaper bureaus and correspondents. There are thousands of national magazines and tens of thousands of national newsletters, all carrying news of interest to a variety of groups.

Lee Loevinger, *Symposium on Media Concentration*, vol. 2, 1978.

As newspaper chains became dominant and as fewer American cities had competing dailies (a trend that continues today), it was natural that critics would conclude that diversity was down and pluralism was threatened. This rather predictable reaction meshes nicely with two well-embedded American values, namely, that (1) *bigness is bad* and (2) *localism is desirable*. . . . No wonder that publisher Frank Muncey, who was known for his cold-hearted business values, raised hackles when he wrote in 1908 that "there is no business that cries so loud for organization and combination as that of newspaper publishing."

Many commentators who are concerned about media concentration and what they think is a decline in media pluralism look at only one variable: the number of newspaper owners. This coupled with the overall decline in the number of newspapers alarms them. Less often do they consider whether group or chain ownership increases or decreases diversity of media content in a given community. Some newspaper chains like Knight-Ridder have a reputation for quality. Their papers are well-edited and have a wide range of columnists and feature material that leave their readers with considerably more variety than some weaker independently owned newspapers. In this instance, strong ownership has real social benefits. Of course, there are also group owners like Thomson and Newhouse that do not have a reputation for quality. I have personally watched two cities (St. Cloud, Minn., and Salem, Ore.) where most knowledgeable observers agree that the Gannett Company's purchase of local newspapers resulted in a strengthened editorial product.

Degree of Pluralism Uncertain

In fairness, though, I will concede that studies of the consequences of chain ownership and concentration paint a mixed portrait of their actual effect on quality and diversity. Generally, though, I believe that the scales tilt slightly toward advantages that come from chain ownership especially with regard to editorial sources such as news services, columns, comics, etc. The record of chain newspapers with regard to editorial page offerings (as seen in endorsements for Presidential candidates) is less impressive. Chain papers, studies show, are more likely to make endorsements than are independent newspapers, but also more likely to endorse the same candidate. There are exceptions, of course, but I would rate the issue here as something of a draw. While independent newspapers, according to a national study with which I was associated, seemed to avoid controversy and thus cheat their readers out of the "diverse local voice" they might expect, the chains seemed to stamp out their presidential endorsement editorials with the same cookie cutter.

Beyond Dailies

If we stopped our inquiry at the newspaper doorstep, I would be hard pressed to make my case for increased pluralism. However, the media world includes much more than newspapers. In fact, fewer and fewer Americans subscribe to or read a daily newspaper and it is obvious that the newspapers play a less important role in our national life than they once did.

What of other media outlets? Do they contribute to diversity and pluralism or not? First, in broadcasting there are several thousand stations and no one can own more than seven A.M., seven F.M., and seven TV stations, thus preventing monopoly control. Broadcast news programming has increased markedly in recent years as local radio and television stations compete in the ratings for supremacy in news as well as entertainment programming. However, broadcast editorializing is still rather sparse and hardly a major source of guidance to the public.

The magazine field is a great source of diversity of ownership and content. While there is some group ownership, the magazine industry has less concentration of ownership than other American industries, including newspapers, and the possibility for new magazines to develop is very great indeed. Although they were the first mass medium in America, magazines no longer court the mass audience to the extent that they once did, but rather try for a quite defined, specialized readership. They want the skier, for example, not a mythical average citizen. This means that the range and diversity of content in magazines is almost limitless, with nearly every possible special interest represented. Magazines also carry a wide variety of opinion ranging from the far left to the far right; some are downright anarchistic. There are critics who argue that this diversity is meaningless because many magazines have relatively small circulations and are therefore not reaching enough people to make a difference. This objection is largely nonsense because a small, respected journal can have enormous impact. A specialized publication like the *New England Journal of Medicine*, which enjoys enormous respect in the medical community, can easily have more influence and impact than a network television show on the same subject by the sheer force of that publication's authoritativeness with an audience that counts. . . .

No Hard Evidence

It is true that many important stories are not published and some of them would be poor publicity for big business. But there is no hard evidence that the choices that must be made to cope with an oversupply of news are dictated by narrow self-interest. In fact, many recent broadcasts, movies, magazines, and newspaper features have carried stories critical of business.

Similarly, the charge that business interests are responsible for the general support by media personnel of the existing political system is not borne out. It seems much more likely that American journalists in large organizations, like their colleagues in small, independently owned enterprises, are interested in appealing to their audiences and so reflect the values of mainstream American society. All of this does not prove that pro-business bias is nonexistent, but it raises some doubts about its nature and extent.

Doris Graber, *Mass Media and American Politics*, 1980.

Finally, the rapidly expanding field of cable communication and other new technologies, such as direct broadcast service, have large promise for diversity and pluralism both because of their varied general offerings and also because of those programs calibrated to specific ethnic groups, subcultures, and interests. In many cities now there are at least 12 available channels, while many others have more than 30 and some will soon have 100 or more. Remember that each channel can be multiplied by the 24 hours in the day which makes the potential for diverse programs quite massive. . . . Cable programmers offer hundreds of possibilities in special programming for women, the aged, ethnic minorities, children, and others. There are specialized sports networks, another that covers Congress, even outlets for soft-porn and much, much more. There are news services offered by Associated Press, Dow Jones, UPI, and Reuters. . . . Before long most cities will also have cable public access channels that will allow local citizens and groups to make their own television programs and present their viewpoints as an alternative to the traditional media fare of the commercial programmers.

All this adds up to a portrait of media diversity both of ownership and of a content that would blow a circuit in the brains of the Framers who worried about keeping newspapers free from governmental licensing and control. In a society where points of view range from serious commentary about foreign affairs to proposals for more nude beaches, there is clearly a good deal of diversity. Even ethnic and cultural subgroups benefit from the communication revolution of the 1980s—both in the traditional media, which are seeking minority audiences, and in new media which are developing programs tailor-made for Blacks, Chicanos, Native Americans, and others.

If we once had reason to worry that national networks and conglomerate control of local newspapers and broadcast stations might lead to a nation of homogenized interests, the electronic revolution, especially as represented by cable, ought to relieve many fears. Naturally, some large firms have moved into this business (Time Inc., for example, owns Home Box Office and Cinemax), but there are still many alternative voices.

Overwhelming Number of Sources

The diverse sources of information and opinion are almost mind boggling. These are with us already in greater numbers than any of us can hope to comprehend, let alone use. The real secret of intellectual survival for the consumer in an information society with these massive offerings lies in understanding the range of possibilities and knowing how to use them to personal advantage. There are, of course, reasons to be concerned about information-rich people vs. information-poor people. Information is power and some information will no doubt be priced so high that it will be out of reach of many people. Even then, though, through the prudent use of libraries and other public sources, most of us will have such enormous choices, so rich and varied, that anyone who suggests that media pluralism is diminishing will look quite silly. Diversity of ownership and content are up, not down.

"We are repeatedly told of scandal, violence, economic disaster, . . . and so on, and not really told of the health and vigor of our society."

The Media's Bad News Bias May Harm Society

Ben J. Wattenberg

What effect do newscasts containing violence, revolution, scandal, and corruption have on society? Critics charge the media, especially television, with concentrating on "bad" news that gives viewers an inaccurate and hopeless view of the world. In the following viewpoint, Ben J. Wattenberg, a nationally-syndicated columnist, argues that the "bad news bias" of the media could have a demoralizing effect on American society if the bias is not reversed.

As you read, consider the following questions:

1. Why does the author compare the press to Typhoid Mary?
2. According to the author, why may the press no longer be able to unify society?
3. In Wattenberg's opinion, what has become the adversary culture in modern America?

Ben J. Wattenberg, *The Good News Is the Bad News Is Wrong.* New York: Simon & Schuster, 1984. Copyright © 1984, 1985 by BJW, Inc. Reprinted permission of SIMON & SCHUSTER, Inc.

Suppose there is a bad news bias. . . .

It may be asked: so what? After all, even if there is a more pervasive, more potent Bad News Bias, we've survived and prospered in so many ways. . . . We still have strong and patriotic values, feisty politics, an improving quality to our lives, a strong economy. What's the problem?

Well, we are a strong society. But it is still altogether proper to ask this: has our strong society been harmed in some ways by the nature of our media system? And further, even more important: is it possible that we will be hurt—perhaps more severely—in the future?

A Modern Typhoid Mary

Recall our early image of the modern press: Typhoid Mary.

Mary, you will recall, was a waitress. Back in 1919, she went about her business, innocently serving her customers crullers and coffee. As it turned out she also served up a little typhoid bacillus with those healthy breakfasts. Some of her customers—days later—got very, very sick with typhoid fever. *Something happened to the customers after exposure.*

We have had a video news explosion in recent years. More news, more dramatically presented, most of it bad news. *Has something happened to us because of the exposure? Is something likely to happen to us because of this exposure?* How are we to judge this?

An informed population, we have all believed almost reflexively, is the bulwark of democracy. Theoretically, a still more informed population is better yet. We do get plenty of straight news. But suppose that so much of the information we are getting—the Distilled Essence of Media on a hundred topics—is wrong, or wrong-headed, or skewed, or misleading? What then? After all, Mary also served nourishing food along with a little bacillus.

Suppose we are repeatedly told of scandal, violence, economic disaster, pollution, licentiousness, and so on, and not really told of the health and vigor of our society. Suppose this bombardment of bad news is increasing in intensity. Suppose, further, that there may be a cumulative effect to the Bad News Bias; a year of bad news may have a small effect, but a decade of it more of an effect, and a generation—still more.

Long Term Effect

If that is what is happening, even in a healthy society, has it hurt us—will it hurt us? Is bad news—incorrect bad news, that is—bad for us?

Well, of course, we don't know, any of us. There are some things that have already happened that may be plausibly linked to the bad-news bacillus. But data about the future are in short supply, and speculation has often yielded famous stupidity. Still, it is important now that we try. There is a lot at stake, as we shall see.

If we do not *know* the future, there are, however, some things about it that seem logical and reasonable, if not necessarily provable. I do not suggest here that we are in for a siege of media-induced typhoid.

There are lesser contagious diseases that can be quite uncomfortable. . . .

Crying Wolf

Consider some of the . . . wages of the Bad News Bias that the media inflict on themselves.

One constructive function of a free press is to galvanize public concern about real ills in society. But if the anchorman cries wolf every evening, and the American people shrug it off as just so much more negativism—whom can anchormen galvanize?

Or try it the other way. Suppose people were to believe all the bad news pumped out by the Bad News Bias. That would in effect go a long way toward destroying a cardinal precept of public policy: "If it ain't broke don't fix it."

Print the Good News

If, in fact, part of our job is to reflect society, to be to some degree a mirror of society, then—and I will get into a lot of trouble in my own craft for saying this—we have an absolute obligation to look for the good as well as for the not-so-good, the good deeds as well as the misdeeds. That is absolutely consistent with honest, aggressive journalism. But what has happened in the smart set among journalists is that bad news is perceived as the only good journalism. I'm not suggesting one should hide the bad news. I am saying that part of the balance of a good newspaper is telling people about things that work in society as well as things that do not work.

David Lawrence, *The Center Magazine*, May/June 1985.

After all, according to the Bad News Bias, everything is broke. The Federal Aviation Administration doesn't enforce safety standards, so planes crash. The Environmental Protection Agency is blind to business violations, so people die of air pollution. If a bridge falls, all bridges are about to fall as the decaying of the American infrastructure proceeds. If there is one instance of police brutality, we are a brutal people. What to do? Everything is broke! Answer: Fix everything!

But you can't fix everything right away. The resources don't exist. Overfixing things that are hardly broke can harm us. Trying to fix everything may mean fixing nothing as arguments break out about priorities.

Do we want to spend another billion on air pollution, if it comes at the expense of, oh, pick any old program, say, food for hungry children?

Do we want to put a heavy negative spotlight on police behavior—to a point where cops become afraid of bad publicity, and are afraid to enforce the law—and somebody's mother gets mugged?

It is not only hungry children and mugged mothers and America that are hurt by this process. The press is hurt in ways that hurt most.

We are speculating. . . . What happens when people come to believe that the press is too negative and *not to be believed*? The press begins to become irrelevant. What could be sadder than an irrelevant anchorman? . . .

When the nightly news starts reporting good news as well as bad news, it will be believed. When the news is credible, we will get more positive action stimulated by bad news. When our news is more realistic, we will get fewer foolish actions stimulated by phony bad news.

That would be good for all of us. And nobody in government would dare lay a glove on the press.

A Demoralizing Factor?

And finally, as we speculate about the future, we ought to face one overarching question: can the Bad News Bias demoralize us?

When all is said and done, a free society does not have much more than belief in itself. Many great modern thinkers (Joseph Schumpeter, for one) have understood this and reached a gloomy conclusion—that a society could be healthy enough, but that an "adversary culture" (as Lionel Trilling called it) or, more recently, a "new class," or "elitists," could be so negative about modern democratic life and its culture that they could (often unwittingly) undermine it, robbing it of its vigor, vitality, and confidence.

Schumpeter wrote about this in 1942, long before television entered our homes and our lives. But television has bolstered his case many fold. He was talking about the influence of intellectuals who wrote in little magazines. But the negative position is now put forward every night in almost every living room. It is fair to ask: will the Bad News Bias of television become the Schumpeterian instrumentality that steals our modern magic away from us?

Will a society that comes to believe it is no longer great have the audacity to send people to the moon and beyond? Will a society that comes to believe nothing works well anymore be able to muster its resources and try to cure cancer? Will a society that is told inferentially every evening that it is no longer proudly riding the wave of history, but is perhaps struggling immorally against the tide, be willing to pay what is necessary to defend its interests and to promote its democratic values? Will a society that believes modernity is a blind alley be prepared to help premodern societies along the road to better health, literacy, communications, economic growth? . . .

The Future of Civilization

Logic tells us that the media blues may have a continuing effect upon us, perhaps at compound interest, as a generation grows up with the magic box in the rec room blaring more and more bad news, told more dramatically and more often than ever before.

We don't any of us know the future. But this is a potentially serious problem and we ought to think about it. The argument is about the nature of and future of our civilization.

"The bad news, however awful, points to the goodness and rationality in the countless events that go unremarked."

Bad News *Is* the News

Colin Morris

Critics of the media often complain that news reporters are preoccupied with death and destruction. Presidents chide the press for negative coverage, religious leaders call for positive stories, and parents often find newscasts too violent and traumatic for young children to watch. Colin Morris, the head of the British Broadcasting Corporation's Religious Broadcasting, defends the newsworthiness of bad news. In the following viewpoint, Morris writes that news consists of unusual events. Since the usual events of society are good, the news must be bad.

As you read, consider the following questions:

1. What is the author's definition of news?
2. According to the author, why is bad news more attention-grabbing than good?
3. In the author's opinion, how is bad news softened when handled by the media?

Colin Morris, "What's So Good About the Bad News," *The Listener*, September 1986. © The Listener.

A television news-reader once confessed to staggering out of the studio after reciting the nightly catalogue of death, disaster, accident and crime, wondering about taking a more cheerful job in an abattoir. And I heard a motherly viewer comment, 'That poor girl is close to tears!' as an apparently disconsolate Jan Leeming [a newscaster] gathered up her papers at the end of another grim news bulletin.

So pervasive is the gloom which seems to shroud all the television news outlets that if any station went berserk and decided to corner the market in cheerful items, dropping the gloomy component of its bulletins, who would believe it? Viewers would probably feel vulnerable because they were not being alerted to the latest disaster looming on the horizon. After all, that dismal world journalists persist in showing us is our world, it's the only one we've got, and if there's something radically wrong with it, then it's our problem.

It seems to me that the issue boils down to a number of practical questions, each of which has something to do with theology. First of all, what is news? Secondly, how does television as a medium handle news? Thirdly, why does bad news have such a morbid fascination for us? Fourthly, and this is as much an assertion as a question, aren't television journalists performing a religious task in the strict meaning of that word when they try to put our experience into some kind of context?

What Is News?

In deciding what is news, I start from a theological premise. The baseline is a normal, happy, well-adjusted society; God's good creation, within which much human existence is routine and unremarkable. News is anything new and interesting which disturbs this state of affairs (the bad news) or reinforces it in striking ways (the good news). What, arguably, is not news is the reiteration of normality, the assertion that all is well in God's creation. That's an important truth, but something which, for the most part, we take for granted, like the fish's assumption that the ocean isn't running short of water. Normality is only news in an abnormal context.

The statement, 'There were no shootings, bombings or incidents of arson in Milton Keynes [England] yesterday', though comforting for the citizens of that town, has little interest for viewers elsewhere. However, substitute 'Beirut' for 'Milton Keynes' and you have news.

Paradoxically, to start from the assumption of a good creation makes a preponderance of bad news inevitable. The bad news, however awful, points to the goodness and rationality in the countless events that go unremarked. Once good news begins to dominate the bulletins then it is a sad, bad world which becomes the norm. Of course, you can stand this argument on its head and take as your baseline an irrational, evil world. But here we've got to make a fundamental moral choice that comes before any discussion about television news. We've got to decide whether evil is a powerful intrusion in a basically good world or goodness an heroic assertion of nobility against the odds in an evil world. We'd be wise to make up our minds on this issue because, as someone has said, he who sits on the fence in the modern world tends to get electrocuted.

A Good World

In practice, the fact that television journalism's vote is cast in favour of a basically good world is signalled by a ritual which is rather like the preacher's rhetorical flourish at the climax to a grim sermon. 'And finally. . . .' says the newscaster on *News at Ten*, heralding an end-of-bulletin story which is guaranteed to be cheerful or even frivolous; designed to send viewers to bed in good spirits—a ringing declaration that at the end of the day things are not all that bad, even though the body of the bulletin has been doom-laden. In the Hollywood western, good triumphs over evil in the final reel; in the television news bulletin it fights its way to the surface through the murk just before sign-off time.

Responsibility of the Press

The press, by its very nature, is rarely beloved. "Nobody," wrote Sophocles, "likes the man who brings bad news." But bringing bad news is one of the primary responsibilities of the press. It has been the press, after all, that has brought its readers and viewers reports of war and disasters, of social and economic turmoil. Americans, whose tolerance for bad news increases in direct proportion to the distance that such news must travel, have long been able to tolerate news of revolutions, famines, floods, and other catastrophes if those events happened in places like Spain, China, or India. But in recent years, the bad news has come from closer to home.

Peter Stoler, *The War Against the Press*, 1986.

Now, the world may indeed be a good creation, but we've learned by hard experience that it's also a dangerous place. I suspect the public's lust for news, which arguably results in more news outlets than there is news to fill them, originates in a sense of psychic insecurity. I'm sure it's unhistorical romanticism to claim that our forebears felt more at home in the world than we do, but at least, unless they were unlucky enough to be living in the eye of the hurricane, happenings far beyond the parish boundary were already merging into history by the time they heard of them.

But now, to paraphrase John Wesley, the whole world is our parish. We need to be reassured, frequently, that things are holding together in those parts of the big world which could affect our little world. So let's put the news on. . . .

Evil Grabs Attention

And when we do put the news on, we have to confess that evil seems to have a decided advantage over good in grabbing our attention. The things that could do me and my little world harm are usually, though not always, more immediate and graphic than the things that might do me good. The effects of goodness often occur beyond the camera's range—in the human heart, for instance. The teenage thug beating up an old lady makes a gripping story (God help us) whereas the saga of that youth's ultimate rehabilitation, should it happen, is likely to be long-drawn-out and outwardly uneventful. It's an important and cheering thing to happen, but it's a process rather than an event; in television terms, it's the difference between filming a tree growing and filming a tornado tearing that tree out of the ground. . . .

Edmund Burke wrote: 'I am convinced that we have a degree of delight, and that no small one, in the real misfortunes and pains of others.' This is one reason why evil in all its manifestations has always been a central theme in popular culture. Those, alas, who demand radical programme changes to banish the darker side of life from our television screens, either in news bulletins or elsewhere, are seeking not so much modifications in broadcasting policy as amendment of human nature. As a preacher I'm all for that, but it's an awful responsibility to load on to the broadcaster.

That old question of natural theology—what evidence is there of God at work is his world?—is given new urgency by what the ordinary viewer can see on his or her television screen. I doubt that the faith of many serious believers is totally undermined by shocking pictures of natural disasters, because they have usually passed beyond any belief in a crudely interventionist God bent on punishing a sinful world. But the problem of convincing the general public about the existence of a good God is made more acute. It takes courage, some might say gall, for preachers and theologians to proclaim God's loving care for his children to a society whose eyes and hearts have just been lacerated by news footage of famine in Ethiopia or the Sudan.

Evil and Love

The believer contends that evil is at all times fearsome, but never overwhelming nor ultimately decisive. It is to be resisted, confounded, beaten back. And television news is a constant witness to this epic confrontation between evil and human love.

We rarely see raw evil depicted in television news, evil out of control, on the rampage; the context is invariably one of challenge and response—gruesome road accident *and* police and ambulance crews; volcanic eruption *and* rescue-workers picking through the rubble; distraught relatives *and* the comfort of friends and neighbours.

That old parable Jesus told us about the wheat and the weeds has a contemporary ring to it. Wheat and weeds, symbolising good and evil, grow together in a field, nurtured by the same sun, watered by the same rain, woven together to the point where they cannot be separated. Until the Harvest. The average news bulletin is a vivid commentary on that parable—morally ambiguous life in history's field on this side of the Harvest.

Reassuring Bad News

From time to time, people complain that the papers don't print any good news. (Presidents, especially, tend to complain about this.) . . . But good news is not a newspaper's job. We don't mean this the way it sounds, in some civics-class, watchdog-of-the-democratic-process, Fourth Estate sense. We mean that psychologically there is something reassuring about the newspaper *because* it is full of bad news—the same bad news each morning.

New Yorker, May 7, 1984.

In the Book of Genesis, it is God who brings order out of chaos; in the modern world, television journalists have to make a stab at doing it. They subdue into harmony a mountain of telex print-outs, miles of video tape and a pandemonium of ringing telephones. They organise into a coherent picture a riot of impressions, a chaos of events, a bedlam of attitudes and opinions that would otherwise send us scurrying to the hills in a panic. And they have to construct this world view at lightning speed, in a welter of instant judgments. Not for them the luxury afforded to philosophers of earlier ages who could reflect at leisure on the fitness of things. Aristotle had no six o'clock deadline to meet.

Distinguishing Bias from Reason

When dealing with controversial issues, many people allow their feelings to dominate their powers of reason. Thus, one of the most important critical thinking skills is the ability to distinguish between statements based upon emotion or bias and conclusions based upon a rational consideration of the facts.

The following statements are taken from the viewpoints in this chapter. Consider each statement carefully. *Mark R for any statement you believe is based on reason or a rational consideration of the facts. Mark B for any statement you believe is based on bias, prejudice, or emotion. Mark I for any statement you think is impossible to judge.*

If you are doing this activity as a member of a class or group, compare your answers with those of other class or group members. Be able to defend your answers. You may discover that others come to different conclusions than you do. Listening to the rationale others present for their answers may give you valuable insights in distinguishing between bias and reason.

> R = *a statement based upon reason*
> B = *a statement based upon bias*
> I = *a statement impossible to·judge*

1. Throughout the 20th century, American journalism has been solidly in the liberal camp.

2. Since journalists have many different sources for their news stories, they are not entirely at the mercy of any single source.

3. Objective reporting has stripped reporters of their creativity and their imagination.

4. Ten huge business and financial corporations control the three major television and radio networks, 59 magazines, and 58 newspapers, thus calling into question the idea of an "independent" press.

5. The First Amendment calls for freedom of speech; therefore, one of its intentions was to allow for diversity of opinion in the media.

6. Members of the media suffer from both ignorance of the world and from a sense of morality that permeates our culture.

7. Ethnic subgroups benefit from the communication revolution of the 1980s which allows for more public access through cable TV.

8. The press has completely accepted the idea of an ongoing East-West struggle.

9. If leaks become widespread, US policy makers may retaliate by excluding the public from public policy decisions.

10. An informed population is the bulwark of democracy.

11. One constructive function of a free press is to inform the public about the ills of society.

12. When reduced to its fundamental features, media pluralism usually means two things: diversity of ownership and diversity of content.

13. When putting on the news, we have to confess that evil has a decided advantage over good in grabbing our attention.

Periodical Bibliography

The following articles have been selected to supplement the diverse views expressed in this chapter.

Ben Bagdikian   "The Media Grab," *Channels of Communications*, May/June 1985.

James Fallows   "The New Celebrities of Washington," *The New York Review of Books*, June 12, 1986.

Herbert Gans   "Are U.S. Journalists Dangerously Liberal?" *Columbia Journalism Review*, November/December 1985.

Thomas Griffith   "The Blanding of Newspapers," *Time*, October 21, 1985.

Harper's   "Can the Press Tell the Truth?" January 1985.

S.L. Harrison   "Prime Time Pablum," *The Washington Monthly*, January 1986.

Christopher Hitchens   "Blabscam," *Harper's*, March 1987.

Michael Massing   "The Rise and Decline of Accuracy in Media," *The Nation*, September 13, 1986.

Abigail McCarthy   "Is Good News News?" *Commonweal*, July 12, 1985.

National Review   "Feeling Bad About Ourselves," May 17, 1985.

Jeffrey Pasley   "Inside Dopes," *The New Republic*, February 23, 1987.

Michael Robinson   "Jesse Helms, Take Stock," *Washington Journalism Review*, April 1985.

Michael Robinson   "Pressing Opinion," *Public Opinion*, September/October 1986.

Herbert Schiller   "Behind the Media Merger Movement," *The Nation*, June 8, 1985.

Vittorio Zucconi   "America's Media Empires," *World Press Review*, May 1986.

2 CHAPTER

Should Government
Regulate the Media?

Chapter Preface

The media perform an awesome task for the American public. They provide sports scores, entertainment guides, human interest stories, and obituaries, and more importantly, they inform citizens of local, state, national, and international news.

Critics of the media believe that it is impossible to provide all this information and at the same time insure the expression of all relevant points of view. They advocate government regulations to guarantee politically-balanced news coverage and to limit the media's power. The measures these critics support include libel laws to protect the reputations of individuals, top-secret classifications to safeguard national security, and rules such as the Fairness Doctrine to insure equal time for opposition groups.

Conversely, civil libertarians argue that democracy can only be insured when media ethics are left to journalists, broadcasters, and the public audience. Anti-regulation groups contend that the government cannot be trusted to provide accurate, unbiased information to the public. Nor can it be trusted to evaluate freedom of speech, they assert. Only by allowing divergent opinions, including those opposed to democracy, can personal freedom be maintained. Civil libertarians argue that more harm is done by regulating the media than by any leak of military secrets or slanderous statements.

As the authors in this chapter demonstrate, both factions want to insure balanced, accurate information in the media, yet the means they offer to do so differ greatly.

"The availability of heavy punitive damages in libel litigation has benefits for a free society."

Libel Laws Serve the Public Interest

Jerome A. Barron

Libel laws were created to protect individuals from slanderous statements made by the press. In 1964 the Supreme Court altered libel laws in a landmark case entitled *The New York Times v. Sullivan*. The court decided that plaintiffs in libel trials not only had to prove that statements were false and defamatory, but that they were printed with malice. Many lawyers object to the decision, but law experts like Jerome A. Barron, dean of the National Law Center at George Washington University, believe the laws are still effective. In the following viewpoint, Barron writes that libel laws allow citizens to protect their reputations from harm caused by the media.

As you read, consider the following questions:

1. According to the author, why do people initiate libel suits?
2. In Barron's opinion, how do punitive damages against the media serve as an equalizer?
3. Why does Barron believe that the media should be held accountable by law?

Jerome A. Barron, "The Search for Media Accountability," *Suffolk University Law Review,* Winter 1985. Reprinted from 19 Suffolk University Law Review, 789 through 814, by permission. Copyright 1985 by Suffolk University.

A number of years ago, I said that the Supreme Court developed the doctrine of *New York Times v. Sullivan* to stimulate debate and to "ensure a courageous press." I asserted that "the opportunity for counterattack ought to be at the very heart of a constitutional theory" concerned with providing individuals with freedom of expression. Instead, *New York Times v. Sullivan* provided the press with a new license for attack, without allowing anyone the opportunity for counterattack.

More than a decade after *New York Times v. Sullivan*, we are still engaged in the same quest—the effort to make free speech a shared, rather than a vicarious, right. Freedom of the press is still too often viewed in our society as a right to be vicariously enjoyed by the public through the mass media. True press freedom is a fundamental value, and its realization should be as important a social objective as the equally important, and sometimes competing, value of protecting the freedom of the institutional media. We should reject the premise that press freedom automatically provides free expression for the entire society. Free expression for all members of society cannot be realized without some measure of media accountability.

The Motivation for Libel Suits

An examination of contemporary libel litigation reveals that a significant number of individuals in our society, believing that they were victimized by the press, are willing to sustain great expense to bring libel suits. These individuals do this with the knowledge that damages obtained at trial are unlikely to survive appeal. In short, they sue even though they lose. Individuals increasingly use libel actions for purposes such as vindication, reprisal, response, and publicity. Much of contemporary libel litigation is a result of these desires and emotions.

The question remains whether the libel suit for damages provides the best vehicle for promoting media accountability. In the recent libel suit which General Sharon brought against *Time Magazine*, Judge Sofaer commented on the fury and anger associated with contemporary libel litigation: "One cannot escape the impression that *Time*, like other libel defendants who can afford to fight, has concluded that its best defense is to inflict as much damage upon plaintiffs in the litigation process as plaintiffs are able to inflict on *Time*." Upon examining some recent libel cases, the objectives of the well-publicized libel plaintiffs are not hard to discern. General Sharon brought suit for libel as much to improve his public image as to protect it. Further, he had an ideological agenda. Indeed, in the libel suit, *Time* claimed that, as a matter of law, General Sharon's "motives in commencing this litigation render him incapable of proving damages." *Time* contended that Sharon "convened his suit to vindicate the State of

Israel and the Jewish people." Further, *Time* alleged that Sharon sued because of a long-held belief "that *Time Magazine* was biased against Israel.". . .

Some commentators argue that punitive damages should be eliminated and libel recoveries limited solely to compensation of actual injuries. Punitive damages are routinely condemned, and much ink has been spilled in the law reviews advocating their speedy abolition. Still the availability of heavy punitive damages in libel litigation has benefits for a free society. Punitive damages enable an individual, ground down by the great engines of mass communication law, to do battle. In this context, punitive damages act as an equalizer. Illustrative of this point is the famous recent libel law case brought by William Tavoulareas, President and Chief Executive Officer of Mobil Oil Corporation, and his son, Peter, against the *Washington Post*. In that case, the Tavoulareases claimed that the *Post* had defamed them by alleging that the senior Tavoulareas "had used his influence to 'set up' his son, Peter, in the shipping business, and then had diverted some of Mobil's shipping business to him." An appeals court panel described the grievances of the Tavoulareases by stating that, "[t]he basic theme of the article was that William Tavoulareas had misused his position and corporate assets to benefit his son." The jury awarded $1,800,000 in punitive damages and $250,000 in compensatory damages to William Tavoulareas against the *Post* defendants. The appeals court's decision to reverse the trial court's judgments' determination does not ensure that the Tavoulareases will in fact receive the large amount of damages awarded by the jury since the district court must now dispose of several post-trial motions. In addition, the United States Court of Appeals for the District of Columbia has granted an en banc hearing to review the appeals court's decision.

The Need for Libel Laws

The public deserves protection against the presently unchecked excesses of the elite media. No other event has contributed so much to the arrogance of the elite media today as the *Sullivan* case; there's a need to explore the possibility of a legislative remedy to restore truth and responsibility to the elite media.

Jesse Helms, *Human Events*, March 30, 1985.

The *Tavoulareas* case highlights the current libel law landscape. The magnitude of the punitive damages in this case discloses the enormous impact such damages can have as a weapon in the libel wars against the media. Some commentators assert that punitive damages menace effective free expression, and urge either their abolition or severe curtailment. . . .

Proposals to preclude punitive damage awards overlook the fact that prayers in complaints for enormous punitive damages attract media attention. Consequently, complainants seeking media coverage pray for enormous damages. In the *Tavoulareas* case, for example, it is clear that absent the extensive punitive damages awarded by the jury, the case would have enjoyed less notoriety. Reformers who wish to limit the libel exposure of media defendants will inevitably confront tremendous pressures from those harboring such powerful publicity motivations.

The media's current assault on libel law reflects a misunderstanding of defamation plaintiffs' motivations. Individuals seeking access to the media view libel law as the only means available to them for self-expression and participation in debate, despite the fact that the libel action for damages is too cumbersome and awkward a legal vehicle to achieve effective participation in the opinion process. In short, the problem is not that libel law exists, but rather that it is increasingly used as an all-purpose means of securing media accountability, while it is rarely suited toward that end.

Since the press is usually the defendant in defamation cases, the media predictably and bitterly proclaim and publicize defects and burdens of contemporary libel law. . . .

Getting Back at the Press

Proposals for reforming libel law are unlikely to succeed because most of them are designed to provide greater press freedom, and would take the teeth out of libel law. Because these proposals fail to provide any additional opportunities for public debate in the media, they do not remove the breeding ground for libel suits— the feeling that the press has acted unfairly and unresponsively. Many of the important libel suits being brought today are instituted not to secure libel damages, but to secure attention and to promote debate. One scholar, reflecting on this matter, tellingly asserts that few libel plaintiffs "sue to win; they can win by suing.". . .

No Alternatives

One final question remains. Why assume that media accountability must or should be achieved through law? In this view, media accountability is best achieved in the marketplace of ideas, rather than in the courtroom. If a particular newspaper or broadcast station engages in defamatory falsehood, the readers, listeners, or viewers will turn away from it. Public reaction, therefore, provides the ultimate accountability.

There are two problems with this reasoning. The first is that the marketplace of ideas may exist in the minds of theorists, but it does not exist in the reality of contemporary mass media. There are many communities in which there are no alternative media of similar stature to the daily newspaper or the local television network affiliate. The local community cannot take its quest for a many-sided look at local issues elsewhere as there is no alternative place to go.

The Right to a Good Reputation

It is wrong to undervalue the fundamental nature of the private individual's right to protect his reputation merely because that right is not explicitly mentioned in the Constitution. . . . All parties to the current debate over the future structure of libel law should recognize that the rights of free speech and press, and the right of the private individual to protect his reputation, are not adversarial but instead symbiotic.

Ronald H. Surkin, *Dickinson Law Review*, Spring 1986.

The second objection to this reasoning is that despite efforts to the contrary, the American legal tradition assumes that media accountability should be achieved through law. The history of defamation law in the United States, England, and Canada is illustrative of this tradition. It is my purpose to stimulate the enrichment of this tradition by urging the creation of a new right of reply remedy for defamation that will honor two of our central legal ideas—the sanctity of reputation and the importance of free expression.

"American libel law manages to achieve the worst of two worlds: It does little to protect reputation. It does much to deter speech."

Libel Laws Do Not Serve the Public Interest

Floyd Abrams

Does the First Amendment, which guarantees free speech, apply to court cases involving libel? Many critics of libel law believe that any restriction on the media inhibits free speech. They argue that the threat of costly lawsuits leads the media to avoid investigative reporting and critical documentaries to protect themselves from expensive lawsuits. In the following viewpoint, Floyd Abrams, a New York lawyer and a specialist in constitutional issues, writes that US libel laws harm both the press and private citizens. Abrams suggests five specific changes to improve libel law.

As you read, consider the following questions:

1. Why does the author call libel law a "mad jumble"?
2. According to Abrams, what effect do the libel laws have on public debate?
3. Why does Abrams suggest that monetary damages in libel suits be limited?

Floyd Abrams, "Why We Should Change the Libel Law," *The New York Times Magazine*, September 29, 1985. Copyright © 1985 by The New York Times Company. Reprinted by permission.

Since the Supreme Court ruled in favor of The New York Times in New York Times v. Sullivan in 1964, no country in the world has offered more legal protection for those wishing to speak out frankly and fearlessly. Yet today, American libel law manages to achieve the worst of two worlds: It does little to protect reputation. It does much to deter speech.

Until Times v. Sullivan—in which L.B. Sullivan, a city official in Montgomery, Ala., sued the paper for printing an advertisement critical of the local police's handling of civil-rights demonstrators—the Supreme Court had rarely heard libel cases. Since 1964, it has decided more than 25 such cases. . . .

A Mad Jumble

For all the attention . . . being paid libel in the courts—including the publicity that attended Gen. William C. Westmoreland's suit against CBS and former Israeli Defense Minister Ariel Sharon's case against Time magazine—too little has been paid to the mad jumble libel has become. Who wins? It depends when you ask. Of cases tried around the country from 1980 through 1984, according to the Libel Defense Resource Center in New York, 70 percent were won at the trial level by those who sued. On appeal, however, the situation was reversed. In 64 percent of the cases, the courts ordered judgment to be entered in favor of the press or ordered a new trial. Altogether, according to a newly published study by the Iowa Libel Research Project, only about 10 percent of the cases brought in the nation from 1974 through 1984 were won by the plaintiffs; another 15 percent were settled, usually without any payment of money.

How much do victorious plaintiffs receive? More than half of all initial libel awards are over $100,000. Yet what juries try to do and what appellate courts permit them to do have little in common. Before 1980, figures from the libel defense center show, only one judgment in American history amounted to more than $1 million; from 1980 through 1984, 20 such judgments have been awarded by trial judges and juries. But the appellate courts have yet to affirm a single one. So far, the largest judgment affirmed by an appeals court has been for $400,000. (Some cases, however, have been settled for far in excess of $400,000.)

The Failure of Libel Laws

If all this makes libel law sound like an odd sort of board game with plenty of excitement but little predictability, consider some of the conclusions of the Iowa study to a different question: Why do people sue? They do not sue, the study says, because they have suffered financial damage, but because they feel emotionally harmed by what was written about them. They do not sue because they wish to obtain large monetary awards, but because they wish "to restore their reputations or to punish the media." Since it is cheap for plaintiffs to sue (almost all agree on a contingency fee with their lawyers that requires no payment unless they win), they sue even though their chances of victory in court are slight. Randall P. Bezanson, a law professor at the University of Iowa and co-author of the Iowa study, concluded that plaintiffs do not "sue to win; they win by suing."

But neither side wins much from the way libel law works today. The law effectively chills both the press and private citizens who wish to speak out on public issues. It does this by imperiling those who cannot afford to risk the possibility of huge court judgments or the certainty of ever-increasing defense fees. From the point of view of most plaintiffs, the law provides a bit of psychic gratification in being in court at all, but little more.

"WE'D BETTER TONE THIS DOWN OR GEORGE III WILL SUE US FOR LIBEL..."

Tony Auth. © 1985, Washington Post Writers Group, reprinted with permission.

The sole purpose of libel law is the restoration of unjustly lost reputation. That intent needs to be brought back into focus. Among the changes that I propose in this article are steps to encourage publishers to print corrections, limits on damages to amounts actually lost by those who sue, and the adoption of a rule providing that the loser in libel cases should generally bear the costs of the case. With changes such as these, we can avoid inhibiting speech while permitting those who should sue to do so. . . .

When libel law is viewed freshly as an effort of the law to permit people to restore their unjustly diminished reputations—

something rarely achieved even with a successful suit—certain conclusions follow as to how the law should be changed. Five changes should be considered:

First, and most important, corrections should be encouraged. If a publication or broadcaster is presented with proof that its report was false and it promptly and prominently corrects the error, no suit should be allowed. As Steven Brill, publisher and editor of The American Lawyer, has written, "Our goal, it should be remembered, is to restore reputations, not punish publications." There could be some provisions for a modest monetary award, even if a correction was published, if the plaintiff had suffered out-of-pocket losses in the interim. But if a correction was promptly and prominently published, the most that should be allowed by way of damages is the actual amount lost by the plaintiff as a result of the initial publication.

Second, the risk of damages should be limited. Libel suits should not resemble lotteries in which the chance of success is minimal but in which the image of last year's lucky winner leads to the purchase of yet another ticket to possible financial independence. Damages for emotional injury should have a ceiling. In California, for example, awards for pain and suffering in medical malpractice cases have been limited to $250,000. There is no reason not to limit recoveries from emotional injury supposedly caused by libel—the sort of injury the Iowa project found was invariably the only kind sustained—to a fixed figure of, say, $100,000. Actual losses of income should be allowed up to their total amount. Punitive damages should be abolished.

Legal Costs

Third, rules about counsel fees should be changed, to add a note of caution to both sides in a libel case. Unlike the British system, in which the losing party always must pay the legal costs of both parties, the American practice has been that each party generally bears its own costs. Our approach has had the salutary effect of opening the courts to more people; the fear of being responsible for costs is one significant factor that deters the less affluent in Britain from suing. In libel cases, courts should be empowered to impose on the losing side the penalty of paying the legal fees of the winning side if a suit was brought or defended without sufficient basis. The rule need not be rigid and could permit judges a good deal of discretion in deciding when costs should be awarded. Still, the rule, not the exception, should be that the loser pays.

Fourth, libel law should be interpreted to permit the harshest commentary on the performance of those in power. This does not mean that the Westmorelands and Sharons of the world should be barred from suing at all. But the concept of what is "opinion" (and thus not subject to a libel suit) should be interpreted most broadly in cases brought by public officials, leaving critics free to attribute evil motives, unworthy purposes and the like to those in power. In South Dakota Governor Janklow's lawsuit against Newsweek, for instance, Judge Richard S. Arnold of the United States Court of Appeals for the Eighth Circuit observed that charges against public officials "that one can hear every day wherever government, state or Federal, is discussed" should be protected under the First Amendment even if they are "ill-tempered or ill-considered." Although "good people may shrink from public office" because of the charges, Judge Arnold wrote, the "framers of our Constitution long ago struck the balance in favor of speech." If Judge Arnold's views are not already the law (and I think they are), they should be.

Libel Suits Squelch Debate

Make no mistake. Libel suits by public officials do not promote diversity, criticism or dissent. To the contrary, they put a heavy price on it. They enforce the power of those who govern. They reduce the power of those who are governed.

The libel problem is real. It is frightening. It is menacing to a nation that has thrived and flourished on vigorous dissent and unfettered criticism of government and its officials.

Eugene L. Roberts Jr., *Update on Law-Related Education*, Fall 1985.

Fifth, a proposal . . . embodied in a study bill introduced by Representative Charles E. Schumer, Democrat of New York, should be considered. . . . The bill, containing variations on ideas first outlined by Marc A. Franklin, a law professor at Stanford University, would permit a public official or public figure who has been the subject of a publication or broadcast to bring an action which does not seek any monetary damages but simply a declaratory judgment that what had been said was false. At the same time, a libel defendant sued for monetary damages by a public person could "convert" the action to one for a declaratory judgment. The principal issue in such cases would be truth; no issues relating to the state of mind of the journalist or the appropriateness of the care taken by the journalist would be considered.

The effect would likely be a major decrease in the cost of and time devoted to individual libel cases as well as the total amount of monetary judgments awarded. At the same time, the proposal might lead to a major increase in the number of libel cases seeking declarations of truth, an increase leading to still more money being spent on libel cases and more time—perhaps too much time—being devoted to them.

Representative Schumer's proposal, thoughtful and innovative as it is, involves a trade-off for both sides in the libel war. Plaintiffs would lose the chance (and defendants, the risk) of monetary damages. Defendants might find themselves, far too often for their comfort, obliged to defend "truth" suits. Although Federal legislation embodying the proposal is now premature, it would be useful for a state or two to enact such legislation to see how the idea works in practice.

Uninhibited and Robust Debate

Finally, the constitutional rules established in Times v. Sullivan should be preserved. Too often in recent years, judicial critics of that ruling have carried the day in writing crabbed and grudging interpretations of that case. In the Times case itself, the Supreme Court observed that the purpose of the First Amendment was to assure that public debate was "uninhibited, robust and wide open." A reversal of the decision would go a long way toward assuring the opposite result.

"There simply has to be much, much more opportunity for people who have differing points of view to be heard on television."

The Fairness Doctrine Aids Freedom of Speech

Neil Hickey

In 1949 the Federal Communications Commission created the Fairness Doctrine to ensure that opposing viewpoints could be heard on the few existing broadcast stations. With the advent of cable TV and the proliferation of independent stations, many critics believe the Fairness Doctrine is no longer needed. Others however, argue that the rule is still needed to protect minority views from being overpowered by corporate broadcasters. In the following viewpoint, Neil Hickey, the chief of *TV Guide's* New York bureau, writes that the networks must allow more time for rebuttal to create a balanced forum of ideas.

As you read, consider the following questions:

1. In the author's opinion, what would networks gain by airing rebuttals?
2. According to Fred Friendly, why are TV documentaries so bland?
3. Why do critics of the networks say that the public is dissatisfied with mass media?

Neil Hickey, "TV *Must* Create Rebuttal Time," *TV Guide*, June 22, 1985. Reprinted with permission from TV GUIDE ® Magazine. Copyright © 1985 by Triangle Publications, Inc. Radnor, Pennsylvania.

On March 9, 1954, Edward R. Murrow went before CBS's cameras and narrated a 30-minute program that denounced the Communist witch-hunt tactics of Sen. Joseph R. McCarthy of Wisconsin. That *See It Now* broadcast is still one of the most famous in television history, contributing significantly, as it did, to McCarthy's eventual decline and fall.

During it, Murrow intoned: "If the senator believes we have done violence to his words or his pictures and desires to speak, to answer himself, an opportunity will be afforded him on this program." McCarthy accepted, CBS News paid the production costs, and four weeks later his half-hour rebuttal was broadcast to the Nation. It was one of the rare instances in the 40-old-year history of American television that any individual or corporation has been handed free air time to reply to a previous broadcast. . . .

And yet, media theorists of the political left, right, and center have long agreed that some mechanism is desperately needed for the systematic access to the airwaves by people who either feel themselves personally wronged by a television program, or who wish to express strong and reasonable opinions in rebuttal to those presented by the broadcaster.

Defuse Anger

If the networks voluntarily awarded such time, the argument goes, then the anger and dismay of aggrieved parties would be defused at an early stage and they might not resort to Fairness Doctrine complaints, which can be prolonged, frustrating and expensive; or to court trials, which can be even *more* prolonged, frustrating and infinitely more expensive. And besides that, say many experts, the networks plainly *owe* their viewership an avenue for the redress of genuine grievances because broadcasters have monopoly usage of a limited natural resource—namely, publicly owned airwaves—from which they derive enormous profits.

Many broadcasters agree there's a need for such a mechanism. Correspondent Mike Wallace, a defendant in the . . . $120-million libel suit brought by Gen. William C. Westmoreland against CBS, says "there has to be a better, more reasonable way [than court action] for public officials, public figures . . . to respond to criticism that they feel is unfair. . . . But we at CBS News have not yet made a sufficient effort to come up with a workable format to permit [it]. And we postpone putting forward such a plan at our own peril. We *cannot* complain about libel trials, and preach the necessity of free and full discussion of issues of public controversy, and then *fail* to make our facilities available for that discussion."

Says Richard Salant, one-time president of CBS News and more recently president of the now-defunct National News Council:

"There simply has to be much, *much* more opportunity for people who have differing points of view to be heard on television."

Another former CBS News president, Fred W. Friendly (now professor emeritus at the Columbia University Graduate School of Journalism), says, "If you have a pressure cooker with no safety valve, you're in trouble. Television has none." That's why so many documentaries are bland, he insists. The striving for total objectivity, in order to head off angry criticism, precludes any strong point of view.

Serving the Public Interest

[The Fairness Doctrine] is the only means now available to assure that diverse and divergent views are broadcast. Without the rule, the business motivations of broadcasters might overwhelm the public interest in the airing of public issues. . . . Broadcasters might only air views with which they agree if they were freed from complying with the rule. Because they are privileged to use the public's airwaves, broadcasters must serve the public interest, including . . . the providing of balanced, fair programming.

Ford Rowan, *Broadcast Fairness*, 1984.

A canvass of the networks for a list of their "response" programs turned up the following: besides its McCarthy broadcast, CBS offered General Westmoreland 15 minutes of unedited air time to respond to its Jan. 23, 1982, *CBS Reports* documentary "The Uncounted Enemy: A Vietnam Deception," which the general said defamed him. Westmoreland turned the offer down, and declined as well to file a "personal-attack" complaint with the FCC. He opted instead for the libel action, and then withdrew it later, somewhat ignominiously, when it appeared the trial was going against him.

Examples

NBC points to a June 19, 1967, documentary called "The JFK Conspiracy: The Case of Jim Garrison," in which the network attacked some theories of the then New Orleans district attorney about how President John F. Kennedy was assassinated. Garrison objected to the broadcast, and a month later on July 15, 1967, he appeared on NBC for 30 minutes to give his side of the story.

NBC also calls attention to an experiment conducted on the *Today* show last March [1985] in which a prominent conservative spokesperson (Terry Dolan, chairman of the National Conservative Political Action Committee [NCPAC], delivered from his own political perspective a news story on the accession of Mikhail Gorbachev to leadership of the Soviet Union. NBC provided him with

85

film footage, a producer, let him write the story his own way and gave him several minutes to present it. Also on *Today*: correspondent Bill Monroe conducts a five-minute segment every other week in which letter-writers are taped, and then shown voicing their complaints on the air.

ABC's claim to right-of-reply fame is its late-night irregularly scheduled *Viewpoint* program that was born amid controversy: Kaiser Aluminum protested to ABC about its treatment in a *20/20* segment, and the very first *Viewpoint* (in prime time), on July 24, 1981, contained a rebuttal by a Kaiser executive. . . .

"Arrogant" Newspeople

That's about it. Partly as a result of the television industry's niggardliness about the right-of-reply issue, a public perception of TV newspeople as being "arrogant" has grown in recent years.

"One of the real underlying roots of public dissatisfaction with mass media is that it's beyond redress," says media observer Hodding Carter 3rd. "I fully understand the difficulties the electronic media have in making adequate time available and choosing between the many voices that want to be heard. But it's not beyond the bounds of their ingenuity and creativity to make it happen."

Similar sentiments come from spokespersons all across the political spectrum. Reed J. Irvine, chairman of AIM [Accuracy in Media], complains there's "almost zero access [to the national networks]. . . . If we had enlightened people running television networks, they would say, 'Let's do this voluntarily. Let's go out of our way to meet with people having legitimate, documented complaints, and let's invite them in to have their say'."

Andrew Jay Schwartzman, executive director of the liberal Media Access Project, says that PBS's action in handing over time to AIM is "appropriate," and he laments that the networks historically have taken "an extremely hard line" on that issue. He may or may not agree with the content of AIM's broadcast, says Schwartzman, "but we are better off that PBS is airing it."

A First Amendment Right

The Rev. Dr. Everett C. Parker, a leader of the citizens' reform movement in broadcasting, says that the right of reply is inherent in the First Amendment—which does not *just* guarantee the free speech of broadcasters but of the public as well, especially vis-á-vis the electronic media, which have monopoly custodianship of the public's own airwaves.

A few tentative solutions are at hand, if the broadcasters choose to adopt them, and many say they are eager to do so. One network news president, Lawrence K. Grossman of NBC, says that there "*are* opportunities to open up the dialogue" with viewers and to serve their "legitimate" desire for access "to what has traditionally been a closed preserve." He'd like to see more "guest pieces" from outside experts: the electronic counterpart of magazine articles by non-staff writers.

Most observers are persuaded that television needs its own version of the Op-Ed page—vigorous opinion across a wide spectrum from many sources, whether in response to real or imagined "personal attack"; or as a corrective to viewpoints purveyed by broadcasters.

A Public Trust

[The Fairness Doctrine] insures that those voices which cannot be heard due to the scarcity of broadcast frequencies are presented. . . . After five decades of operation the broadcast industry does not seem to have grasped the simple fact that a broadcasting license is a public trust subject to termination for breach of duty.

Media Access Project petitioners, quoted in *Broadcasting*, October 13, 1986.

Indeed, the networks ought to seek out contrary viewpoints rather than wait to be challenged. And, of course, the broadcasters themselves should be the organizers, the traffic cops and the editors, weeding out the frivolous requests for time from the thoughtful ones.

Talk Back to Television

Fred Friendly goes so far as to suggest that PBS should air a one-hour weekly program—paid for by the commercial networks and stations—that would be a national soapbox for viewers with a gripe or a grudge about the media. "Self-examination, indeed, constant vigilance," he says, "appears far more necessary today than ever and for reasons that are far more complex than simply explaining ourselves to a mistrusting public."

Talking back to television is an idea whose time came many years ago. All that remains is for television people to have the grit, the will and the commitment to make it finally happen.

"In an era of many sources of news and information, how sensible is it to require each TV station to balance its news and public affairs shows?"

The Fairness Doctrine Hinders Freedom of Speech

Hugh Carter Donahue

The US Constitution protects freedom of speech for all Americans. Why, then, would many broadcast journalists want to eradicate the Fairness Doctrine, a law that guarantees equal time for opposing viewpoints? Critics oppose the law because they believe it creates timid newscasters, bland documentaries, and huge legal costs. In the following viewpoint, Hugh Carter Donahue, assistant professor of journalism at Ohio State University, writes that the Fairness Doctrine is outdated by advances in mass media technology and is misused by special interest groups to promote their views.

As you read, consider the following questions:

1. According to the author, what requirements does the Fairness Doctrine impose on newscasts?
2. Why does Donahue believe that providing equal time encourages censorship?
3. In the author's opinion, how does the Fairness Doctrine affect news coverage?

Television and radio inform us about the pressing issues we face: the deficit, the arms race, the homeless, the shift from manufacturing to service, the latest political scandals, South Africa's deepening chaos, drunken drivers, and insider trading on Wall Street, to name a few. The list goes on, almost as 24-hour all-news programming does. Every weekday night 38 million Americans watch one of the network newcasts, and 4 million watch public television's "MacNeil/Lehrer Newshour." The Cable News Network reaches 700,000 viewers with around-the-clock service daily, while 80 percent of all Americans listen to the news over their radios.

For nearly 200 years the First Amendment of the Bill of Rights has protected speech from government censorship. The amendment states simply that "Congress shall make no law respecting an establishment of religion, or prohibiting the free expression thereof; or abridging the freedom of speech, or the press; or the right of the people peaceably to assemble, and to petition the Government for a redress of grievances."

Of course, laws and court decisions do place some limitations on speech. One may not libel another individual with impunity or cry "Fire!" in a crowded theater where there is no fire. But in general a person may voice any opinion, no matter how seemingly outrageous, and allege any fact, no matter how universally disputed. Those who framed the Constitution believed that as long as government was prohibited from censorship, diverse voices would present a variety of views to the public.

However, special rules apply for television and radio news broadcasts, as well as for public-affairs programs, which provide analysis or in-depth coverage of timely public issues. Since 1949 the Federal Communications Commission (FCC) has regulated these forms of speech through the Fairness Doctrine, which imposes two requirements. First, broadcasters must air controversial news and public-affairs programming. If viewers or listeners believe programming is not fair, they can petition the FCC to instruct broadcasters to cover stories and issues differently. Second, the Fairness Doctrine demands that broadcasters give organizations and individuals airtime to respond to editorials and to commercials on public issues. If a broadcaster sells time to advocates of a balanced budget, opponents of a balanced budget must receive time, too. And if none of them will pay for that time, the broadcaster must donate it. Comparable regulation for print would be unthinkable.

Spectrum Scarcity

The Fairness Doctrine rests on the technological grounds of "spectrum scarcity." The number of radio and television channels is limited, since each has to have exclusive use of a certain amount of bandwidth—a certain range of frequencies—within the portion of the electromagnetic spectrum suitable for broadcast.

The rationale is that there are more people who wish to operate television and radio stations than there are available channels. So the broadcaster becomes a public trustee with a government license to use a scarce resource. Members of the community cannot simply start stations to broadcast their own views, as they might presumably start a small newspaper. Instead, the Fairness Doctrine requires each broadcaster to provide access to individuals and organizations. The audience is sovereign of the airwaves, and the government measures the diversity of speech by looking at the individual broadcaster, not the sum of all broadcasters.

A Doctrine of Censorship

The marketplace of ideas is too important to be subject to the blue grease pencil of the censor. As a democratic society we should recognize when we have strayed from the principles of free speech and press. The fairness doctrine is an aberration in our tradition of free expression and should be abolished.

Mark S. Fowler, *Washington Post*, February 25, 1986.

Despite its apparently beneficent purposes, the Fairness Doctrine is Orwellian. This novel inversion of First Amendment rights shifts protection from speakers—radio and television broadcasters—to listeners. It does not seek to prevent government censorship. Rather, the overriding concern is to ensure that people are exposed to divergent viewpoints. While the First Amendment keeps the government out of the business of regulating speech, the effect of the Fairness Doctrine is to put the government squarely in that business.

Pushing Agendas

The results are predictable. Interest groups can push their agendas, and administrations can threaten to revoke licenses if they dislike coverage. According to Floyd Abrams, a prominent First Amendment attorney and NBC's lawyer, administrations going back to Kennedy have attempted to exert pressure on broadcasters through the FCC. He charges that in 1984 and 1985 the CIA attempted to use the Fairness Doctrine to challenge ABC's coverage of an alleged CIA plot to assassinate a former agent.

Though designed to increase the variety of views aired, the Fairness Doctrine in practice achieves the opposite effect. Producers become timorous, reluctant to face conflicting demands for reply time and government complaints about fairness violations. FCC Commissioner James H. Quello, who opposes the

Fairness Doctrine, has described an incident that occurred when he was general manager of WJAR Radio in Detroit. In 1960 his station ran editorials in favor of fluoridation but granted an anti-fluoridation advocate a chance to voice a rebuttal. Medical and dental experts lodged a sheaf of criticisms, saying that the station had confused the public, and Quello had to agree. The station ended up dropping editorializing entirely to avoid Fairness Doctrine controversies.

When there were few radio and TV stations, and their ownership was concentrated in large corporations, it may have appeared reasonable to require community access to broadcast technology, despite all the problems that approach entails. However, the number of television and radio stations have increased enormously, and cable television, satellite broadcasts, low-power television, and other new communications technologies have proliferated. More and more producers can provide a wide range of radio and television news programs. It is time to give broadcasting the same First Amendment rights that the print media enjoy.

The Political Controversy

Interest groups that battle each other on virtually all other issues close ranks behind the Fairness Doctrine. Supporters include big business such as General Motors and Mobil; Phyllis Schlafly's right-wing Eagle Forum; Accuracy in Media, a group committed to ending journalism's allegedly liberal bias; the National Rifle Association; labor organizations; the Anti-Defamation League of B'nai B'rith; the NAACP; and the Democratic Party.

All contend that the Fairness Doctrine is not excessively intrusive. They believe it is merely remedial, allowing imbalances in news coverage to be corrected and granting interested individuals and organizations an opportunity to respond to editorial views. To be sure, broadcasters live with the threat of losing lucrative licenses should they fail to comply. But Fairness Doctrine proponents point out that between 1980 and 1986, when over 132 cases of unfairness were alleged, the FCC ruled against only 20 broadcasters. The commission dismissed many more cases as unworthy of review.

The proponents use the Fairness Doctrine to advance their particular causes. Phyllis Schlafly, who opposes the Equal Rights Amendment (ERA), claims that the Fairness Doctrine gives her the power to arrange for negative news coverage of this issue. "Of all the TV coverage on the ERA, over 95 percent was pro-ERA and only 5 percent of it was against the ERA. If it weren't for the Fairness Doctrine, we couldn't have gotten even that measly 5 percent," she said in 1985, during hearings the FCC conducted on the Fairness Doctrine. At the same hearings, a B'nai B'rith attorney claimed that the Fairness Doctrine helps fight anti-Semitism in small towns with few radio and no television stations. But then he clumsily acknowledged that B'nai B'rith had used the Fairness Doctrine to negotiate network coverage of the 1982 Israeli invasion of Lebanon.

Misuse of Equal Time

Mobil praised the Fairness Doctrine for enabling it to go after broadcasters whose news reports of the giant oil company have been critical. That freedom is important to Mobil since many broadcasters refuse to carry its public-message commercials. They do so not out of any special love for the little guy but because the Fairness Doctrine obligates them to air opposing public-interest advertisements even if no one will pay for the time. Anti-nuclear advocates suppressed ads for a New York power plant by bringing a Fairness Doctrine complaint to the FCC.

A Sword of Damocles

In spite of the fact that the FCC has shown moderation in putting it to use, the very fact that the . . . [Fairness] doctrine confers on a government agency the power to sit in judgment over news broadcasts makes it a tempting device for use by any administration in power to influence the content of broadcast journalism.

William S. Paley, quoted in *Mass Media Law and Regulation*, 1986.

Some might ask why TV stations shouldn't provide forums for interest groups. Aren't the groups using the doctrine just as it was intended? However questionable some of the viewpoints might seem, doesn't the flow of information to the public stimulate debate?

Of course, television should provide interesting, informative programming. But in an era of many sources of news and information, how sensible is it to require each TV station to balance its news and public affairs shows? Should individual broadcasters have to bend news programming to accommodate specific interests? Wouldn't more intelligent policy give broadcasters the same First Amendment rights as print journalists? Broadcasters already worry lest their news programming offend their audience and jeopardize advertising revenues. The Fairness Doctrine merely aggravates the problem. Broadcasters purvey the uncontroversial to forestall the relentless stream of interest-group demands.

Chills, Stifles, and Inhibits

Broadcasters, journalists, and broadcasting trade groups say that the Fairness Doctrine chills news coverage, stifles controversial public-affairs programming, and inhibits editorials. CBS anchor

Dan Rather commented for the 1985 FCC inquiry, "When I was a young reporter, I worked briefly for the wire services, small radio stations, and newspapers, and I finally settled into a job at a large radio station owned by the *Houston Chronicle*. Almost immediately on starting work in that station's newsroom, I became aware of a concern which I had previously barely known existed—the FCC. The journalists at the *Chronicle* did not worry about it; those at the radio station did. Not only the station manager but the newspeople as well were very much aware of this government presence looking over their shoulders. I can recall newsroom conversations about what the FCC implications of broadcasting a particular story would be. Once a newsperson has to stop and consider what a government agency will think of something he or she wants to put on the air, an invaluable element of freedom has been lost."

"The print-anything-you-can-steal ethic is just plain wrong."

National Security Is Harmed by the Press

Raymond Price and M. Stanton Evans

During his first term in office, President Reagan rebuked the media for their irresponsibility in printing sensitive information. This public scathing failed to change media practices. In Part I of the following two-part viewpoint, Raymond Price, a nationally-syndicated columnist, argues that media personnel lose their perspective on stories due to intense competition. In Part II, M. Stanton Evans, also a nationally-syndicated columnist, writes that journalists must police themselves before they do serious harm to national security.

As you read, consider the following questions:

1. Price writes that the government must restrict the flow of information. What does he think the press should do?
2. Why does the author say the public has a "right not to know"?
3. Why does Evans argue that the prohibition of journalists in Grenada was justified?

Raymond Price, "The Right Not to Know," *The Washington Times*, May 29, 1986. Reprinted with permission from the New York Times Sales Syndication Corporation.
M. Stanton Evans, "Print Anything You Can Steal," *The Washington Times*, November 6, 1985. Reprinted with permission from Heritage Features Syndicate.

I

In every editor's desk there is a drawer full of overwrought images ready for the next dust-up between press and government. The typical drawer holds the messenger killed for bringing bad news, a dozen chilling effects, and 27,373 solemn invocations of the public's right to know. Behind the Spiro Agnew voodoo doll is an ominous veil of secrecy. There's a box of denigrating quotation marks to put around "national security." And the warning that, as one broadcast executive put it recently, "You never know when you're being victimized, that maybe this is the first step in a move by this or any other administration to shut down the press."

The latest emptying of the drawers was touched off by [former] CIA director William Casey's threat to prosecute several news organizations for violating a law banning publication of certain sensitive intelligence secrets.

Leaks are a real problem, but what we need is neither prosecution for newsmen nor polygraph tests for suspected sources. These steps are offensive and probably counterproductive. What we do need is a return to restraint and responsibility on both sides.

Prying Information

The press always argues that if there is a problem, it is with the person who leaks the information. Up to a point, this is true. Many officials and staff members do rush to the telephone the moment they learn something hot. But among reporters, one of the most prized professional skills is the ability to pry information out of people who don't want to divulge it. If the government needs to clean up its act, exercising greater discipline over the loose flow of information, the press also needs to clean up its act in terms of the kinds of information it goes after and the means by which it does so.

Some things simply shouldn't be reported.

Shortly after I joined the White House staff in 1969, I had lunch with two prominent members of the Washington press corps. One was a former colleague from the *New York Herald Tribune*. After the initial pleasantries, my former colleague led into the subject of Vietnam. He pressed me with questions about what President Nixon planned to do next: what new concessions would we offer diplomatically, what moves would we make militarily, if the path we were on didn't lead where we hoped? He wheedled, he bludgeoned, he demanded; and when I persisted in telling him nothing, he exploded in anger.

If I hadn't been stubborn, he could have had a good story. It might have cost lives on the battlefield, and it would certainly have compromised the peace negotiations. But he would have had something his competitors didn't and, by the ethics of his world, that was what mattered. In the business of shoplifting secrets, he operated by the shoplifter's code.

If reporters and editors showed the same degree of restraint we expect from schoolchildren in a candy store when the owner's back is turned, the problem of truly damaging leaks would largely solve itself.

Most of these are not the "government's" secrets. They're the nation's secrets—yours, mine, the people's. The reporter who tries to pry them out so he can score against the competition by splashing them across Page 1 is committing an offense against each and every one of us. It's as simple and as basic as that.

Steve Kelley, reprinted with permission.

It's not that newsmen rushing secrets into print are deliberately betraying their country. They don't see it that way at all. They're simply following the imperatives of their craft as reinterpreted during the counterculture wave of the 1960s and '70s. That's when draft-card burning was in vogue, and when trendy publications offered instructions on making Molotov cocktails. Government was the enemy, and the Pentagon represented the heart of darkness. That's also when the notion took hold that good journalism was "adversary" journalism, with the government to be held guilty until proven innocent.

Wall Street brokers go to jail for trading on inside information. In that business, it's recognized that some information needs to be kept private until the appropriate time. Most government secrets fall into the category of information that is harmful if disclosed prematurely or partially. Some secrets are inherently sensitive, regardless of timing. In either case, it's the public's interests that are at risk in the disclosure.

As citizens, we do have a "right to know" certain things. But we also have a right not to know others. That is, we should insist on respect for a certain right of collective privacy, so that the part of our public business that depends on privacy for its conduct can be conducted in private.

II

Among its other effects, the Pentagon Papers-Watergate era gave us a brand-new principle of journalistic ethics: it's all right to publish anything that you can steal.

An especially troublesome example of this practice popped up . . . in *The Washington Post*—a lengthy story concerning official plans to launch a "covert action" campaign against Libyan dictator Muammar Qaddafi. *The Post* devoted some 45 column-inches to exposing this endeavor, including direct quotations from a "top secret" report from the CIA.

The harm that publication of such material can do to our security interests—and the propaganda bonus it provides our enemies—are obvious on the face of it. That our government (and others) ought to take action against Qaddafi and his global terror network can hardly be doubted. Yet *The Post* had no compunction about blowing this operation in the name of journalistic enterprise.

Can't Keep Secrets

This performance by *The Post* confirms in retrospect the wisdom of the official decision . . . not to invite the media along to the invasion of Grenada. There were numerous protests at the time that journalists could be counted on to keep security secrets, a la World War II. The Qaddafi episode—along with some other . . . happenings—shows otherwise. . . .

In terms of media and official conduct alike, we now are paying the price for the anti-intelligence frenzy of the middle-1970s. In that period, in a supposed effort to remedy abuses, we eviscerated the CIA, hamstrung the FBI, destroyed most of our other security safeguards, and enshrined the notion that anything and everything done by our security/intelligence agencies was fair game for exposure.

I am no knee-jerk apologist for the CIA. When in my view the agency (or a faction within it) has erred, . . . [I have] said so. But it should be apparent to anyone with a modicum of knowledge about the world we live in that we urgently need such an agency, and that much of what it does must be kept secret if it is to be effective.

This is particularly so when we reflect that our adversaries include not only the likes of Qaddafi, but the Soviet KGB and various of its East-bloc henchmen. These practitioners of terror, espionage, and disinformation must laugh up their sleeves when elements in our government and media torpedo an operation like the plan against Qaddafi.

Plugging the Leaks

Given our laws, it is unlikely anyone can or will do anything to *The Post* for publishing these damaging revelations. Nor is this the proper way to approach the matter. Far more to the point is the need to go to the source. The Reagan administation has been plagued by leaks on matters of this type, and many others. Those leaks need plugging. The intelligence committees of Congress are pledged to secrecy on such matters. They should take steps to ensure that pledge is honored.

As for the media, it is time for people in this business to take stock of what we're doing. There is indeed a public "right to know" about the activities of government, and in many cases we should be doing a better job of protecting that right than is now the case.

But blowing authentic national security operations is another matter. In this context, the print-anything-you-can-steal ethic is just plain wrong, and journalists should say so.

"The press must continue its mission of publishing information that it—and it alone— determines to be in the public interest . . . serving society, not government."

National Security Is Not Harmed by the Press

Benjamin C. Bradlee

Since the advent of newspapers, reporters have printed secret information (leaks) provided by government officials. Journalists often defend this practice by citing the public's "right to know." In the following viewpoint, Benjamin C. Bradlee, executive editor of *The Washington Post*, writes that reporters can incorporate leaks in their stories without damaging national security.

As you read, consider the following questions:

1. How do editors of *The Washington Post* deal with national security issues in their paper, according to the author?
2. In Bradlee's opinion, why does the Pelton spy case prove that journalists can keep a secret?
3. The author describes "weapons of the press" which provide a green light to print sensitive stories. What are they?

Benjamin C. Bradlee, "The Press Is Not Reckless About National Security," *The Washington Post National Weekly Edition*, June 23, 1986. Reprinted with permission.

National security means protection or defense of the country against attack, sedition, espionage or other forms of hostile interference. It isn't a complicated concept.

It isn't just hard to be against national security; it's inconceivable.

And yet, why is the director of Central Intelligence trying to get various news organizations indicted for the treasonous disclosure of information classified in the interest of national security? Why does the director of the National Security Agency threaten to prosecute news organizations if they publish information he thinks threatens the national security? What does the assistant to the president for national security affairs have in mind when he joins the battle with such relish?

Why is the president of the United States himself so concerned that he calls the chairman of the board of this newspaper and asks that information be withheld in the interest of national security?

What's all the fuss about? Do these men really think the people who run this newspaper would betray their country? What reporter and what editor could betray this trust, and look their owner in their eye?

It sounds so simple, but it isn't.

Stormy Debates

The Washington Post has been at the center of some stormy national security debates in the last 20 years. One of those debates—the Pentagon Papers—went all the way to the Supreme Court in 1971 before it was resolved, in favor of the press. . . .

The most anguishing of these debates surrounds the story we published . . . about the Ronald Pelton spy case, after eight months of internal discussion and six months of conversations with the highest government officials.

As usual, outsiders seem both fascinated and mystified by how this newspaper handles this kind of story.

The Pelton case illustrates two important points about how The Post deals with national security issues:

• First, we do consult with the government regularly about sensitive stories and we do withhold stories for national security reasons, far more often than the public might think. . . .

• Second, we don't allow the government—or anyone else—to decide what we should print. That is our job, and doing it responsibly is what a free press is all about.

Trouble starts when people try to sweep a lot of garbage under the rug of national security. Even some very highly placed people.

Like President Richard Nixon in 1969, when he described a New York Times exclusive report on the secret bombing of Cambodia as an egregious example of national security violation.

That's right out of Kafka, when you think about it. The Cambodians certainly knew they were being bombed, and since only the United States was then flying bombing missions in Indochina, they certainly knew who was bombing them. If the Cambodians knew, the Vietcong knew. And if the Vietcong knew, their Soviet allies knew immediately. So what was all that about? Well, the American people didn't know and, in fact they had been told we would not bomb Cambodia.

Here, national security was used to cover up a national embarrassment: The president had lied to the American people and to the world. But the New York Times story, by William Beecher, was used by the White House to justify creation of the infamous Plumbers unit, ostensibly to plug the leak that produced this dreadful violation of national security.

This led us to Watergate, of course. Is there anyone now alive and kicking in today's national security debate who remembers Nixon looking the world in its television eye and telling us he couldn't tell the world the truth about Watergate because national security was involved?

The worst lie of all.

Harmful Secrecy

The First Amendment was written, and some of those who wrote it said so, in order to provide a means for exposing the secrets of government. Our government was founded by people who didn't trust government unchecked, unhindered, and unrestrained, and who wrote the First Amendment with the precise idea that things kept secret tend to fester inside the government, and are not very good for the country. While excessive disclosure has on occasion hurt this country, I would submit that excessive secrecy has been much more harmful.

Daniel Schorr, *Harper's*, November 1985.

All of this is not to say that there is no such thing as a legitimate claim of national security. Of course there is, and this newspaper does keep information out of print for reasons of national security. I can't give you a list without violating the national-security interest that led me to withhold publication.

Withheld Stories

In addition to stories that are withheld for reasons of national security, there are some close calls—stories that are eventually run, after long discussions where opposing views are vigorously defended.

Such a story appeared in The Washington Post on Feb. 18, 1977, under the headline "CIA Paid Millions to Jordan's King Hussein," and under reporter Bob Woodward's byline. Millions of dollars of "walking around money" (as distinct from economic or military aid) had been paid to the king by the CIA under the codeword project name "No Beef."

Jimmy Carter had been president less than a month. He agreed to see Woodward and me, after we sought White House reaction to the story before publication. The president totally disarmed us by admitting the story was true. He said the payments had been stopped, and then stunned us by saying that he had known nothing about it until The Post has sought White House reaction, despite multiple briefings during the preceding months by outgoing Secretary of State Henry Kissinger and CIA Director George Bush. The president never asked that the story not be printed, although he made clear he hoped it would not. He told us that the story, if printed, would make the progress he hoped for in the Middle East harder to achieve.

The argument over whether to print or not to print was spirited, to understate it. Some of us believed that the national interest would best be served if the world knew that the CIA had a king on its payroll and that neither the outgoing CIA director nor the outgoing secretary of State thought that fact was important enough to share with the new president. Others believed that anything that might make resolution of the problems of the Middle East more difficult was not worth the candle of publishing.

No Absolutes

There are no absolutes in such discussions. Rightness or wrongness lies in the eye of the beholder. Our decision was to publish. Hussein is still king. Bush is the vice president, Carter is the former president.

Under President Reagan, there was only one major point of tension about national security between the White House and this newspaper during the first term. It is hard to say whether this period of comparative detente was the result of the presence in the White House of James Baker as chief of staff and David Gergen as director of communications, both now laboring in different vineyards, or the absence of Washington Post interest in national security matters. The latter seems unlikely.

The one incident occurred in December 1984, the waning days of the first term and involved Secretary of Defense Caspar W. Weinberger. The story stemmed from an extraordinary briefing at the Pentagon by Air Force Brig. Gen. Richard F. Abel about the next Discovery space shuttle mission carrying an intelligence satellite. "Speculation" by news organizations on military aspects of the mission would result in a Defense Department investigation, Abel said.

Reporter Walter Pincus was asked casually by one of his editors,

"What the hell is in that satellite, anyway?" He said he would "make a few calls" to find out. Two days and three telephone calls later, a story appeared under his and Mary Thornton's byline, describing in general terms its signals-intelligence mission.

On that same morning, Weinberger was en route to a CNN early morning talk show interview, where he intended to push the Defense Department budget, which was already under a certain amount of attack from the Congress. He was interrupted by CBS reporter Reid Collins and asked if The Post's story "gave aid and comfort to the enemy" (an odd question, it seemed then and now). Weinberger replied that the story did just that, and the fat was in the fire.

Public Information

The Post issued a statement saying that there was nothing in the Pincus-Thornton story that had not appeared in bits and pieces somewhere else. But the damage was done. More than 4,000 letters to the editor were received. Some of the letters contained threats of bodily harm, even death.

No Harmful Results

For all the talk that FOIA [Freedom of Information Act] disclosures have disrupted criminal investigations, encouraged industrial espionage or even allowed foreign powers to obtain national security secrets, FOIA's critics have offered few, if any, examples of government documents that were released with harmful results under the Freedom of Information Act.

On the other hand, there are numerous examples of stories the American people would never have learned about their own government, if journalists, public interest organizations and individual citizens could not use FOIA to obtain government documents.

David Kusnet and Steve Katz, *Champaign-Urbana News-Gazette*, October 8, 1986.

The story would die there, a minor if scarring skirmish in the battle over national security, were it not for a lecture given at Emory University a few days later by Gen. Abel. The general was asked if The Post had violated national security by publishing. He replied that The Post's story contained little or no information not on the public record. No Post reporter was present at the lecture, but a student called the paper to report both the question and the answer. We smelled a hoax, and asked to listen to a tape. We listened. He said it. We still wanted confirmation from Abel, and finally got it at 9 p.m., when he returned to his home from Atlanta.

In September 1985, reporter Woodward came into my office, shut the door, and in almost a whisper laid out an amazing top-secret American intelligence capability that emerged in bits and pieces eight months later in the trial of Ronald Pelton. Woodward described in great detail how the communication intercept had worked, where the communications were intercepted, every detail except Pelton's name.

Woodward didn't have Pelton's name because no American knew for sure at that point that a man named Pelton had sold this intelligence gold mine to the Russians five years earlier. That didn't start to surface until well after Vitaly Yurchenko defected [in 1985] . . . and fingered Pelton. Yurchenko had been Pelton's first KGB contact, the man who had arranged for Pelton to spill the beans. Pelton was arrested Nov. 24, [1985].

But without knowledge of Pelton, back in September, The Washington Post had no knowledge that every detail of our story was already known to the Russians. We thought we had the highest national security secret any of us had ever heard. There was never a thought given to publishing any of this information.

At one of our weekly breakfasts, I told publisher Donald E. Graham about the story, and about my concern that while the administration was beating the press upside the head for run-of-the-mill leaks, truly important national-security information was floating around town. I wondered out loud to him about trying to get an appointment with Reagan to inform him of our information and our concern. We scrapped the idea on the grounds that it would inevitably appear to be self-serving and grandstanding.

Concern Over Leaks

About that time I did run into the president's national security adviser, Vice Adm. John Poindexter, at a dinner party, and asked him for an appointment to discuss the same subject. We did meet, and he suggested I talk to Lt. Gen. William Odom, the head of the National Security Agency. Odom and I first met at his downtown Washington office on Dec. 5, 1985. Post Managing Editor Leonard Downie and two members of Odom's staff also were present. We told the NSA chief the detailed information we had, information we said that the Russians now had as a result of Pelton's treason. We said we felt extremely uncomfortable with this information, but we had it, the Russians had it, and we asked why it should be kept from the American people.

Odom shook his head in dismay. He said the information was still extremely sensitive. We didn't know exactly what the Russions knew, he said. It was hoped, he said, that Pelton would plead guilty, avoiding any public discussion of the evidence against him. He looked us in the eye and told us that any story about this case would gravely threaten the national security of the United States.

We were to hear that claim many, many times in the next five months, as we tried to frame a story that would tell the American people what the Russians already knew—and only what the Russians already knew.

We were determined not to violate the legitimate security of the nation, but we were equally determined not to be browbeaten by the administration, which has from time to time appeared to relish press-bashing, into not publishing something that our enemies already knew.

Red Lights/Green Lights

The weapons of any administration in this kind of battle are formidable: presidents, admirals, generals, CIA directors telling you that publication would endanger the nation and the lives of some of its fighters, and ultimately threatening to prosecute you for violating the law.

These are red lights that a newspaper goes through only with a deliberate lack of speed.

The weapons of the press in this kind of battle are generally the reporters themselves and their facts, the First Amendment and common sense.

These are the green lights that make democracy the greatest form of government yet devised. . . .

Role of the Media

The role of a newspaper in a free society is what is at issue here. Governments prefer a press that makes their job easier, a press that allows them to proceed with minimum public accountability, a press that accepts their version of events with minimum questioning, a press than can be led to the greenest pastures of history by persuasion and manipulation.

In moments of stress between government and the press—and these moments have come and gone since Thomas Jefferson—the government looks for ways to control the press, to eliminate or to minimize the press as an obstacle in the implementation of policy or the solution of problems.

In these moments, especially, the press must continue its mission of publishing information that it—and it alone—determines to be in the public interest, in a useful, timely and responsible manner—serving society, not government.

a critical thinking activity

Ranking Media Values

This activity will allow you to rank the values you believe to be most important to the mass media. In studying the media, you will discover that people have differing opinions on the values that should guide media ethics. For instance, one newspaper publisher may see her publication as a business venture and run it for the purpose of turning a profit. Conversely, a second publisher may wish to uncover the "truth" by printing articles that might offend certain advertisers or readers who support the paper. Both people want to produce the best newspaper possible, yet their underlying values contrast so greatly that their two newspapers would be radically different.

The authors in this chapter offer several suggestions on the ethical standards they believe would create a respected, informative media. Some analysts think that America's media often over-emphasize the negative without justification. Others, however, believe the media are not critical enough when it comes to analyzing the news.

Part I

Step 1. The class should break into groups of four to six students. Each group should rank the media values listed below as though the group ran a national TV network. Use 1 to designate the most important concern, 2 for the second most important concern, and so on.

The media should:

_____ cover news important to the community
_____ attempt complete objectivity
_____ report on stories that may reflect poorly on the government
_____ seek the truth
_____ provide space for advertisers
_____ promote a particular political viewpoint
_____ cover world affairs
_____ be entertaining
_____ provide public service announcements
_____ influence public opinion
_____ be profitable
_____ support the existing political system
_____ allow for opposing opinions

Part II

Step 1. Working within the same group, rank the media values as though the group works for an independent communist newspaper that advocates political change in America.

Step 2. After your group has come to a consensus, compare your answers with those of other groups in a classwide discussion.

Step 3. Then the entire class should discuss the following questions.

1. What media values did the class deem most important from the network TV perspective? Why?
2. What media values did the class deem most important from the communist newspaper perspective? Why?
3. How do you explain the differences?
4. How would you rank the media values?

Periodical Bibliography

The following articles have been selected to supplement the diverse views expressed in this chapter.

Fred Barnes	"Leak Soup," *The New Republic*, May 26, 1986.
Bert R. Briller	"Television and the Free Press Issue," *USA Today*, September 1986.
William T. Casey	"Our National Secrets," *Vital Speeches of the Day*, December 1, 1986.
Mario M. Cuomo	"A Brief on the Freedom of the Press," *Vital Speeches of the Day*, February 5, 1987.
H. Dorfman	"Fighting the Fairness Doctrine," *New Leader*, November 17, 1986.
Rowland Evans and Robert Novak	"Congress Is Crippling the CIA," *Reader's Digest*, November 1986.
M. Garbus	"The Many Costs of Libel," *Publishers Weekly*, September 5, 1986.
William Giles	"Media Leaks: A Two-Way Street," *American Legion Magazine*, November 1986.
Stephen Hess	"Leaks and Other Information Communications," *Society*, January/February 1985.
Robert Jesse	"How Not To Protect Communications," *The New York Times*, September 13, 1986.
Michael Ledeen	"Bums," *The American Spectator*, September 1986.
The Nation	"Truth and Libel," November 1, 1986.
Daniel L. Ritchie	"Promises To Keep," *Vital Speeches of the Day*, November 1, 1983.
Herb Schmertz	"The Friends of Libel Move To Defend the Lie," *Conservative Chronicle*, April 8, 1987.
Dale Van Atta	"The Death of the State Secret," *The New Republic*, February 18, 1985.
The Wall Street Journal	"Fairness Flimflam," April 2, 1987.
The Wall Street Journal	"Freedom Doctrine," September 24, 1986.

What Influence Do the Media Have on Society?

the MASS MEDIA

Chapter Preface

The media are omnipresent in American society. From morning radio disc jockeys to television's David Letterman at midnight, the media provide non-stop programs of entertainment and information for their audiences. Some critics argue that the media emphasize sex and violence and undermine America's moral values. Others, however, believe that Americans are expert media consumers who can decipher myth from reality in their entertainment and news.

According to groups like Accuracy in Media (AIM) and the Parents' Music Resource Center (PMRC), the media's influence is detrimental to the future of America. They argue that the media's liberal, humanist bias has a negative effect on the nation's values. They maintain that just as *Mr. Rogers' Neighborhood* and *The Electric Company* can teach children to count and read, so too can *Miami Vice* and *Dynasty* romanticize violence and promiscuous sex.

Organizations opposed to government regulation of the media, such as People for the American Way (PAW), call the efforts of AIM and PMRC to restrict media a form of censorship. They argue that the media's influence is unproven and that individuals, not the government, should decide which programming is acceptable and which is not.

As the media continue to multiply through cable television and local and national publications, the issue of mass media's influence will remain crucial to American society.

"The media's power is seen in its degrading influence not only on the nation's morals, but on . . . virtually every area of life."

The Media's Influence Undermines America's Morals

Tim LaHaye

Ninety-eight percent of all American homes have a television. In America, there are more radios than people. One cannot walk down a busy US city street without seeing billboards, newspaper stands, and numerous advertisements. What effect do these media messages have on the public? Tim LaHaye, a conservative Christian spokesperson and author, argues that the mass media are destroying America's traditional moral values. In the following viewpoint, LaHaye writes that the media are partially responsible for suicide, divorce, anti-patriotism, and America's defeat in Vietnam.

As you read, consider the following questions:

1. According to the author, how are the media destroying America's moral fabric?
2. What examples of imitative behavior does LaHaye use to prove the media's power?
3. In LaHaye's opinion, why are media producers responsible for sexual immorality and violence?

It is almost impossible to exaggerate the power of the media. We measure power by its effects on those who use it. Who can deny that television, movies, and secular radio programming are having an oppressively harmful influence on the morals of America? Soap operas depict a hedonistic life-style that dramatically and grippingly shows no respect for traditional moral values, and thus appears as the norm to a nation of viewers. On TV homosexuality achieves a respectability that is questionable biblically and historically. Divorce is rendered commonplace, until it is imitated by 51 percent of those who marry.

Although the media producers, whether print, magazine, or electronic, continually say, "We're only giving the people what they want," they are really fabricating what the media producers and owners believe in and advocate. That amoral, and in some cases immoral, philosophy is gradually destroying our nation's moral fabric. The media's power is seen in its degrading influence not only on the nation's morals, but on everything else: national defense, the environment, nuclear power, economics, and virtually every area of life.

Media Influence

For example, World War II comes to mind. The minute Japan bombed Pearl Harbor, the media launched a national defense campaign and whipped the American patriotic spirit into such a frenzy that we attacked both Japan and Germany at nearly the same time, even though they were in opposite parts of the world. Taking the offensive against the Japanese and Germans was possible because it coincided with the ideology of the media molders, who to this day continually subject us to reliving the atrocities of Hitler and the Japanese through TV, movies, books, and articles. Unfortunately our media molders show very little enthusiasm for whipping up a patriotic spirit regarding the spread of Communism anywhere in the world. We perceive the true colors of the media molders by the way they ignore or play down Communism's atrocities and promote the idealism of Communism, in opposition to the realities of history. The powerful might of the American military was defeated in both Korea and Vietnam by the drumbeating attacks of our liberal media. Vietnam stands as a national disgrace, not because we could not win, but because the media so intimidated our national leaders that they would not let us win. Any tactical movements that threatened to provide victory for our military in Vietnam were vilified by the press, until right was made to look wrong and vice versa.

The media never forgave Congressman Richard Nixon for his part in the conviction of Alger Hiss as a Communist. Therefore, his blundering mistakes of Watergate gave them the opportunity they had long awaited—to publicly humiliate and disgrace him.

President Lyndon Baines Johnson, the fair-haired boy of the media during his first term of office, defied them and showed military strength in Vietnam. Ultimately the liberal Texas politician was so intimidated by media demanding United States withdrawal from Vietnam that he declined to run for a second term.

President Jimmy Carter was swept into office largely due to the hype of the media. Never in my lifetime has a committed liberal politician been made to look more like a conservative in order to get elected. But even a favorable media in 1976 could not cover his liberal appointments, administrative incompetence, and lack of leadership ability.

Don Meredith, reprinted with permission.

The biggest disappointment to the liberals of the media during the past fifty years must surely have been the election of Ronald Reagan in 1980. They did everything they could to discredit him, but America's yearning for a strong leader overcame their best efforts. However, they have incessantly criticized and increasingly protested every major decision, and they will do everything in their power to circumvent his valiant attempts to bring America back to traditional moral values, a vibrant economy, and a strong defense policy. . . .

The awesome power of the media is evident in its ability to provoke imitations of the behavior depicted on the screen or in the press.

In January of 1983, David P. Phillips, a professor of sociology at the University of California in San Diego, released his study on the response of television viewers to seven suicide reports between 1972 and 1976. He correlated the day-to-day suicide rates between 1972 and 1976, trying to determine if suicides increased after a major suicide report.

Phillips stated, "For a very brief period of time, U.S. suicides increase significantly just after the appearance of a non-fictional suicide story carried by the network evening news." He reported that following each suicide story, the increase was about twenty-eight deaths per story nationwide in the week following. He based his study on suicide figures provided by the National Center of Health Statistics.

Phillips has also explored what is called "imitative suicide." Earlier research has shown that fatal, single-car crashes also increase after major news stories on suicides and that people will kill themselves after viewing a soap-opera character who commits suicide on the show. Phillips observed, "Taken together, all of these findings support the hypothesis that publicized suicides trigger imitative behavior, sometimes this behavior is overt (in the form of an explicit suicide) and sometimes covert (in the form of automobile or airplane accidents)."

What causes people to imitate the behavior they see on TV? Phillips doesn't really know. "What is it that makes somebody want to buy something that's advertised on television when a prestigious or impressive individual is shown using it? Who knows why that is? . . . I think what's going on in advertising is an artificial form of what's going on in the stuff I'm studying, which is, you might say, national advertising."

Real Life Examples

There are many examples of the media serving as a catalyst for either antisocial or self-destructive behavior. For example, since the movie *The Deer Hunter* began playing in theaters in 1979, at least twenty-five viewers have reenacted the Russian roulette scene in the movie and have blown their brains out. . . .

Ted Turner, owner of Cable News Network and WTBS in Atlanta, is livid about the sex and violence on TV and in our movies. He was particularly disturbed about *The Deer Hunter*. ". . . There was not one single documented example anywhere in Vietnam where the Vietnamese forced Americans to blow their brains out," said Turner. "That was just dreamed up. As if the war wasn't bad enough!"

In San Diego a high-school honor student watched an ABC movie on the life of Lizzie Borden, the notorious ax murderer of the 1890s. Shortly after that he hacked his mother, father, and sister to death. His surviving brother must live the rest of his life

114

as a quadriplegic.

Then, of course, there's John Hinckley, Jr., the young man who attempted to murder President Reagan in 1981. Hinckley had become obsessed with teenage actress Jodi Foster after watching the movie *Taxi*. In this movie, Robert de Niro played the role of a psychopath who became a vigilante and killed people to "protect" Jodi Foster. Hinckley was apparently inspired to kill President Reagan after watching the film.

Altering Beliefs

A single 30-minute exposure to TV can significantly alter basic beliefs, related attitudes and behavior of large numbers of people for at least several months.

Sandra J. Ball-Rokeach, Milton Rokeach, and Joel W. Grube, *Psychology Today*, November 1984.

It is my conviction that moviemakers, producers of TV programming, and far too many journalists are provoking sexual immorality and violence in our society by continuing to graphically portray sex and violence in the media. Those who control the media act irresponsibly in the exercise of their right of free speech. They apparently have no conception of the difference between *liberty* and *license*. The media moguls wield immense power, yet this power is being used to destroy our culture, concepts of right and wrong, and family ties.

Somehow our masters of the media who demand the freedom to express their ideas must be made to realize that they bear the responsibility of the abuse of freedom. Freedom without responsibility always leads to chaos. The ultimate end of unrestrained freedom in media will be a society destroyed by anarchy.

"The mass media are less powerful or autonomous than their critics fear."

The Media's Influence Is Limited

Albert E. Gollin

In colonial times, American mass media consisted of town criers and local newspapers. Since then, the American media have become varied and complex. First came radio, then network television, and now in an age of advancing technology, cable television. Many media analysts believe these diverse channels of communication provide a mirror for American values and interests. In the following viewpoint, Albert E. Gollin, the vice president of research at the Newspaper Advertising Bureau, writes that the diversity of mass media reduce their power to persuade the American public. Rather, Gollin argues, the public influences media content through ratings, box office receipts, and subscription revenue.

As you read, consider the following questions:

1. How does the author argue that media content is not the same as media effect?
2. According to the author, why are media audiences difficult to persuade?
3. In Gollin's opinion, why will media influence always remain small?

Albert E. Gollin, a presentation at the Smithsonian Institution's symposium, "The Road After 1984: High Technology and Human Freedom," in a session on "Can the Mass Media Control Our Thoughts?" Reprinted with the author's permission.

There are several key assumptions underlying prevailing beliefs about media power. It is useful to recall that concern about the effects of the mass media is rooted in the seeming success of propaganda efforts conducted during World War I, and by Nazi and Soviet regimes subsequently, to mobilize, coerce or control their own citizens. More recently, the agenda of concerns has broadened, without wholly losing the edge of anxiety that characterized discussions in that earlier era. Here are just a few examples of questions that have been raised.

- Has the graphic treatment of sex and violence by the media contributed to a decline of morality and trivialized or vulgarized significant aspects of human experience?
- Has the aggressive handling and criticism of political and economic elites by the media eroded their leadership mandates and led to a general decline in the perceived legitimacy of social institutions?
- Are the media persistently exploited for political and commercial purposes, selling us candidates and products we otherwise would not buy?
- Have the media created a popular culture that has steadily cheapened public taste—"sitcoms" and soap operas instead of Shakespeare and Verdi, Harlequin romances instead of Hemingway?
- Did the news media drive Richard Nixon from office, and did they cost us victory in Vietnam?

The list goes on and on. It might be noted in this regard that the criticisms and questions raised are far from consistent internally or devoid of special-interest motives.

Mistaken Assumption

Evidence from mass communication research provides a basis for commenting on several mistaken assumptions made by media critics and others who believe in the media's power to affect our thoughts and actions and to shape our society in various ways, good and bad.

The first of these assumptions is the equating of media content with media effects. In this view, what people see, read or hear—especially when they are repeatedly exposed to the content—actually has the effects one hopes for, or fears, depending upon one's own assessment of a particular message. Based on this simplified stimulus-response conception, for example, are the following convictions:

- Violence in children's TV programming leads to violence on the playground.
- Sexually permissive norms highlighted in films, on television, or in books and magazines are echoed in the behavior of those

exposed to such erotic content.

- Sympathetic portrayals of minorities generate compassion and tolerance.
- Media-based campaigns to reduce energy consumption or to get people to lead healthier lives will yield socially desirable results.

Linked with the equating of content with effects is another assumption: that the *intent* of the communicator is faithfully captured in the responses of those exposed to the message. Thus, according to this view, "M*A*S*H" not only entertains, it also successfully conveys the anti-war intent of its producers. Or Archie Bunker's bigotry, rather than giving sanction to prejudiced attitudes, is perceived as misguided, out of date, and morally reprehensible.

Limiting Media Messages

The evidence from communications research, while admittedly uneven and less than conclusive, nevertheless portrays a set of relationships between the content or intent of media messages and their effects that are more complex and variable in nature. People bring to their encounters with the mass media a formidable array of established habits, motives, social values and perceptual defenses that screen out, derail the intent or limit the force of media messages. The media certainly do affect people in obvious and subtle ways. But no simple 1:1 relationship exists between content and intent and effects.

Reinforcing Your Values

Television's role in changing attitudes and values is governed in large part by selective perception. As a result, television is most successful at reinforcing existing attitudes. Reinforcement is by far the most common effect; after all, since you continually expose yourself to messages congruent with your existing interests and opinions, then you continually affirm those interests and opinions.

F. Leslie Smith, *Perspectives on Radio and Television*, 1979.

Moreover, while media audiences are massive in size—a precondition for mass persuasion—they are socially differentiated, self-selective, often inattentive, and in general—to use a term once employed by Raymond Bauer of Harvard University—'obstinate.' As targets they are elusive and hard to please or to convince. People actively use the media for a wide variety of shared and individual purposes. People are not readily used *by* the media. Why is it, then, that we believe that others in the viewing or reading public are more gullible or passive than we ourselves?

Another assumption often held is that the mass media now operate in an unrestrained fashion, and that their autonomy is a prime source of their power. But media publics not only are individually resistant to the content offered them, in free societies they also significantly affect content through the operation of various feedback mechanisms. In this connection, one has only to recall the decisive role of broadcast ratings, film box-office receipts, subscription and circulation revenues, and the like as market forces that constrain the predilections of media operators and producers. To these "bottom-line" influences one must add the constant stream of criticism, letters and phone calls, self-criticism based on professional values that include service to the public, legal restraints, and the results of marketing studies that seek to discover public tastes, preferences and needs.

Thus, in various direct and indirect ways, the public acts upon the mass media rather than simply being influenced by them. And with the variety of content choices and exposure opportunities expanding steadily, thanks to new communications technologies, the likelihood of successful mass persuasion by the media diminishes still further.

This last point bears upon the initial reception of new technologies, including each of the mass media. As a new type of technology emerges, it is often met by either or both of two sharply contrasting reactions. The first of these is aptly symbolized by the image of the cornucopia—the horn of plenty. The new technology is hailed for its potential benefits—enriching people's lives, removing burdens and contributing to human progress. The contrasting perspective is symbolized by the image of the juggernaut—the machine that is unstoppable, crippling or constraining human freedom.

Most technologies, the mass media included, rarely fulfill either set of extravagant hopes or fears. As they diffuse and become integrated into societies, they change things in the process of extending human capacities. But so too do new forms of art, law, scientific knowledge, war and modes of social organization. Only with hindsight, and often with great difficulty, does it become possible to assess which of these has affected society more broadly and decisively, especially when it comes to human freedom.

Media Diversity

To sum up, while at times unquestionably guilty of harmful excess and error, the mass media are less powerful or autonomous than their critics fear—or than their own agents sometimes like to believe. Media publics are far from compliant or passive, and they are becoming increasingly less so as media choices multiply.

Finally, to contradict Ralph Waldo Emerson, things are not in the saddle, riding humankind. Given the existence of media diversity and continuing feedback from the public, the risks of media-fostered political or cultural hegemony remain small.

In any case, such risks are inseparable from those intrinsic to the functioning of free societies, in which the media now play a variety of indispensable roles.

"Rock has so often been involved in these things [violence, teen suicide, etc.] many of us in psychiatry have had to take it more seriously."

Rock Music Has a Negative Effect on Youth

Rob Lamp

In 1985 the Parents' Music Resource Center [PMRC] succeeded in persuading some record companies to put warning labels on albums the PMRC deemed offensive. The PMRC maintains that parents have a right to know about the sex and violence in the music their children buy. Critics of the PMRC decry these actions as an attempt to censor free speech. In the following viewpoint, Rob Lamp, editor of *Rock Music Update*, writes that rock music is partially responsible for a rise in teen suicides and pregnancies. He also argues that violence depicted in rock music, particularly in videos, inspires adolescents to commit violent acts.

As you read, consider the following questions:

1. According to the author, how can rock music be tied to witchcraft, death, and suicide?
2. In Lamp's opinion, how do rock videos contribute to violence among students?
3. What effect does the author believe rock stars like Madonna and Sheila E. have had on teenage girls?

Rob Lamp, "The World of 'Dark Rock,'" *The New American*, February 17, 1986. Reprinted with permission.

On October 27, 1984, nineteen-year-old John McCollum shot himself in the head in his father's home in Indio, California. According to the coroner's report, McCollum committed suicide "while listening to devil music.". . .

More than a year later, Jack McCollum, the dead youth's father, . . . filed suit against a British heavy metal rock musician, Ozzy Osbourne, and his two record companies, CBS Records and Jet Records. McCollum charge[d] that his son's decision to kill himself was precipitated by listening to an Ozzy Osbourne song "Suicide Solution."

CBS Records released Osbourne's albums "with the knowledge that such would, or at the very least, could promote suicide," McCollum's lawyer Thomas Anderson told a California news conference. . . . Anderson said the suit seeks unspecified compensatory and punitive damages that could amount to millions of dollars.

"The record companies and rock stars know exactly what effect this type of music has on young people," Jack McCollum insisted to reporters. "They know they are encouraging young people to commit suicide."

Of course, Ozzy Osbourne has disputed McCollum's charges. "These comments are slanderous; they are preposterous and . . . ludicrous allegations made against an artist who clearly had nothing remotely related to such thoughts in mind when writing or performing his songs," said Howard Weitzman, Osbourne's attorney.

A Misinterpretation?

Osbourne, former lead singer for the band Black Sabbath, says that McCollum and his lawyer have misinterpreted the meaning of his song. "This song wasn't written for suicide, it was anti-suicide," he said.

"It was about a friend of mine (Bon Scott, lead singer of the heavy metal group AC-DC) who killed himself on alcohol and drugs," Osbourne continued. "It means suicide solution as a liquid; not as a solution or a way out."

Yet, despite the claims of Ozzy Osbourne, the suicide of John McCollum is another link in the chain tying certain types of rock music to incidents of witchcraft, death and suicide across the nation. For example, the names of Ozzy Osbourne and his former band, Black Sabbath, were found spray-painted along with satanic symbols in Northport, New York—the scene of the mutilation-slaying of seventeen-year-old Gary Lauwers. Charged with the murder was seventeen-year-old Richard Kasso, who was reported to be involved in drugs, séances, animal sacrifices, grave digging and other satanic activities.

Attorney William Keahon, who investigated the murder,

reported a strong correlation between the tragic events surrounding the murder and the satanic image of certain rock performers. Keahon admitted: "I look at it as a reasonable person; I know what I see in these rock videos, and I know what I see and hear from these kids who watch these videos and do these drugs. I believe there is an acting out of the same outrageous behavior as what the kids see up there on the stage."

Dark Rock

It is no wonder that parent groups, psychologists, and even some recording artists are reacting strongly against what some are calling "dark rock." Critics identify dark rock as popular music that promotes violent and sexually explicit messages in the lyrics. No longer heard by only a few, these pervasive messages have now crept into the mainstream of American music and are constantly blaring through the stereos of vulnerable teen and pre-teen listeners.

No one blames rock music entirely for the 300 percent rise in adolescent suicides or the seven percent increase in teenage pregnancies. There are certainly many causes for these social problems. However, many observers have become convinced that po-

Steve Kelley, reprinted with permission.

tent messages "aimed" at children that promote and glorify suicide, rape, and sadomasochism at least have to be considered a possible "contributing factor."

Ozzy Osbourne once defended himself to *Circus* magazine by protesting, "As much as the kids love to hear me sing, 'Satan is Lord' and 'I Love You Devil,' I am no satanist—I'm a rock 'n roll rebel." The rock star's wife and manager, Sharon Osbourne, explains: "Ozzy isn't into Satanism . . . that's a marketing campaign we invented for him. He doesn't take it seriously."

But Kerry Livgren, former guitarist for the band Kansas, admits that teenagers do take what he and others say in their music quite seriously. "I've run across many people who worshipped our band and other bands," Livgren commented. "When it got to the point with Kansas when I realized what I was writing in my songs was becoming an actual standard by which people lived—that thousands of kids were looking to me as if I was some type of guru—I knew it had gotten way out of my hands."

Many professionals who study adolescent behavior have been sobered by the effects of dark rock on their patients. Dr. David Guttman, Professor of Psychiatry at Northwestern University told the *Washington Post*, "Rock has so often been involved in these things [violence, teen suicide, etc.] many of us in psychiatry have had to take it more seriously."

Dr. Joseph Novello, a psychiatrist and director of "Gateway," a drug treatment center in Washington, DC, often asks teenagers what kind of music they listen to. "It's clear that kids define themselves to a large extent by the artists and music that they like," says Novello. "There is a small and vulnerable group of youngsters who are inclined to drug abuse who tend to identify with the heavy metal and satanic kind of music."

Rock Videos

Other psychiatrists have cited rock videos as contributors to the rise of violence among students. Thomas Radecki, chairman for the National Coalition on Television Violence (NCTV), estimated that 45 percent of some 1200 rock videos monitored were of a violent nature.

A large number of rock videos were rated "extremely violent" by the NCTV. For example, the Rolling Stones amputation video entitled "Too Much Blood" is a take-off of the Texas Chainsaw Massacre. "They sing about chopping a woman's head off, putting her pieces in the refrigerator, then taking them out and eating them," Radecki commented.

A similar theme appears in Tom Petty's music video, "Don't Come Around Here No More." In it, a woman turns into a cake which Petty slices up with a knife while she is screaming. The final scene shows Petty putting the last piece of cake in his mouth and then burping. "That type of image is really quite harmful. It endorses a hostility and revengeful type of thinking between the sexes," Radecki warns.

In another video by Twisted Sister entitled "We're Not Gonna Take It," a boy decides he's not going to put up with an angry father, so he hurls Dad out the window. Proponents have said that these videos are just tongue-in-cheek or cartoon-like. Unfortunately, a young man in New Mexico took Twisted Sister somewhat seriously when he murdered his father in a similar fashion. The homicide was reported to have been inspired by the Twisted Sister video.

"No Place Here"

Sexuality has always been a part of rock 'n' roll and always will be. Rock 'n' roll is a wonderful genre, very creative. But the people who are responsible lovers of rock 'n' roll ought to be speaking out against . . . the sado-masochism, the violence, the exploitation of women creeping into the genre. People should be talking about it. It's something that no one should condone. The people in the rock 'n' roll industry—all lovers of rock 'n' roll—should say, "This has no place here." Particularly since it is going to younger kids.

Tipper Gore, *The Washington Times*, October 1, 1985.

Scientific research also backs up the assertion that violent videos can have harmful effects on their young viewers. In various surveys done with college students, Dr. Radecki reported a "desensitizing of individuals who watch violent videos."

Advertisers certainly enjoy rock stars like Michael Jackson endorsing their soft drinks. Pepsi paid Jackson $5 million to say "This is the Pepsi Generation." That fantasy helped Pepsi spurt to a $20 million gain in sales [in 1985]. . . . Radecki concludes, "If the little thirty- and sixty-second commercials can sell, certainly the three- and four-minute videos themselves—which are really promoting things of violence, making them seem fun and acceptable, normal, and healthy—will be much more influential."

Sexual Themes

Not only has violence and occult activity become prevalent in today's dark rock, but sexual themes have moved from mere innuendos to blatant profanity.

[We would prefer to end any discussion of eroticism in rock lyrics by simply noting that it exists—abundantly. But that would fail to show the reader how perverse an influence it is on its young audiences. With apologies for the offensive nature, therefore, some less extreme examples follow.—Ed., *New American*.]

Sexuality in popular music has come a long way from Cole Porter's "Birds do it; bees do it. . . ." Popular top forty artists like Cindy Lauper in her song "She Bop" encourage masturbation for teenagers. In "She Bop," Lauper tells her adolescent followers that it won't make you blind and "there ain't no law against it yet."

Prince, described by *Rolling Stone* magazine as the most influential musician of the 1980s, has crossed lines that once were considered taboo in rock. In one of his earlier albums, "Dirty Minds," Prince sings about incest in his song called "Sister" and oral sex in another song entitled "Head."

His film, *Purple Rain*, was a box-office smash and crowned him as rock's new king of sex. Although Prince has toned down his erotic image since the days of "Dirty Minds," he did not completely lose his sexual taint in *Purple Rain*. In the film, Prince thrusts the stage with his body and sings about "a girl named Nikki . . . a sex fiend" who he "met . . . in a hotel lobby masturbating."

Madonna was voted in some polls as the top female performer of 1985. Her hit single, "Like a Virgin," was number one on *Billboard's* list of The Top One Hundred Songs for the year. Her nude photos in *Playboy* and *Penthouse* and her confessions to *Time* magazine reveal that a virgin she is not.

Rock's Sexual Pressure

Madonna-style clothing and accessories are very popular among young girls. Her exposed belly button and "Boy Toy" belt buckle are standard trademarks of the Madonna image. Kendis Moore counsels pregnant teenagers in the Los Angeles area. She told the *Los Angeles Times*, "I know how impressionable these girls are. Rock stars like Madonna, Sheila E., and Vanity are important to them. They buy their records, sing their songs, and dress like them. They get the message of what it means to have sex, and it puts a lot of pressure on them to live up to that image."

The Kinsey Report discovered that, in 1940, 33 percent of all women lost their virginity by age 25. Today, 30 percent have lost it before age sixteen. According to the *Journal of Sex Research*, most women in the 1980s have their first sexual experience between the ages of sixteen and nineteen. A rock magazine headline described the situation appropriately, "The Sexual Revolution is Over! (Sex Won)." . . .

Record companies, like other providers of entertainment, have learned that "sex and violence sells," and this is still the bottom line. Most observers recognize that it is the parents who must take control of the situation and determine what is healthy and unhealthy music for their children.

"If you really want to shield kids from sex and violence . . . everything *better have a warning label on it."*

Rock Music's Effect Is Exaggerated

Leo N. Miletich

Rock music has inspired controversy since Elvis Presley's suggestive hip gyrations during the 1950s. In the 1980s, performers such as Prince, Mötley Crüe, and the Beastie Boys reignited the outcry against rock music's lyrical content. Supporters of the music argue that sexually explicit or violent lyrics have little or no effect on listeners. In the following viewpoint, Leo N. Miletich, a free-lance writer and former disc jockey, writes that music has been attacked as subversive to good morals for centuries. In his opinion, any attempt to label or limit rock lyrics is censorship.

As you read, consider the following questions:

1. Why does the author give examples of controversy over music through the centuries?
2. In Miletich's opinion, what had a more disastrous influence on public morality—Watergate or rock music?
3. According to the author, what would happen if society tried to shield everyone from sex and violence?

Leo N. Miletich, "Rock Me with a Steady Roll." Reprinted, with permission, from the March 1987 issue of REASON magazine. Copyright © 1987 by the Reason Foundation, 2716 Ocean Park Blvd., Suite 1062, Santa Monica, CA 90405.

Music hath more than the power to charm wild beasts; according to some people, it can drive the beast in you wild.

After Jimmy Swaggart denounced Wal-Mart stores in a televised sermon condemning rock music, Wal-Mart leaped on the bluenose bandwagon. Just days later—and less than two weeks after the Meese pornography commission's call for a porn purge—Wal-Mart ordered the removal of certain records and rock-oriented magazines (including *Rolling Stone*) from its 900 stores.

Wal-Mart spokesmen later said Swaggart had nothing to do with the decision, though the company did ask for a copy of the sermon and Swaggart relishes taking responsibility for this moral enlightenment. (As in the case of 7-Eleven and other convenience stores being browbeaten into removing *Playboy* and *Penthouse* from their racks, intimidation tactics often reveal deep reservoirs of timidity among the nation's retailers.)

The . . . knee-jerk, overreactive surge of antimusic mania, fueled by preachers, "concerned parents," and exploitive politicians, may seem like something dreadfully new, a threat unparalleled in world history. In fact, the hysteria is as old as music itself. As Tolstoy said: "The older generation almost always fails to understand the younger one—they think their own immutable values the only ones. . . . And so the older generation barks like a dog at what they don't understand." The barking has been going on a long time.

Lyrics: Past

In the fourth century before Christ, Greek historian Ephorus warned, "Music was invented to deceive and delude mankind." This suspicion is reflected in the works of Aristotle ("The flute is not an instrument which has a good moral effect; it is too exciting") and Plato ("Musical innovation is full of danger to the State, for when modes of music change, the laws of the State always change with them"). The centuries that followed featured variations on those themes.

In 1572 a Vienna ordinance on public dancing laid down the law: "Ladies and maidens are to compose themselves with chastity and modesty and the male persons are to refrain from whirling and other such frivolities."

By 1595 "voluptuous turning, jumping, or running hither and yon" were also banned. (Apparently, "hither" was snuggling somewhere beneath the bandstand while "yon" was out in the dark Vienna woods.) A sermon of the time denounced dancers for "letting themselves be swung around and allowing themselves to be kissed and mauled about. . . . They cannot be honest while each entices the other to harlotry and offers a sop to the devil."

In *A Short View of the Immorality and Profaneness of the English Stage,* Jeremy Collier (1650-1726) decreed that "Musick is almost as dangerous as Gunpowder; and it may be requires looking

Berke Breathed. © 1985, Washington Post Writers Group, reprinted with permission.

after. . . . 'Tis possible a publick Regulation might not be amiss.''

And in *An Irreverent and Thoroughly Incomplete Social History of Almost Everything*, Frank Muir describes the effect of the waltz when it was introduced into England from Germany in 1812: "Guardians of public morality immediately pronounced the waltz to be 'will-corrupting,' 'disgusting,' 'immodest'; an 'outright romp in which the couples not only embrace throughout the dance but, flushed and palpitating, whirl about in the posture of copulation.'''

In 1957, Meredith Wilson's *The Music Man* had Professor Harold Hill warning the people of River City, Iowa, about the evils inherent in ragtime (but you'll have to go listen to the record; permission to quote the passage was denied). Contemporary audiences laughed, but in fact, ragtime—perhaps because of its origins in bawdyhouse parlors, performed by itinerant black musicians like Jelly Roll Morton and Scott Joplin—was no joke at the turn of the century. . . .

In 1986 the parents of a teenage boy who killed himself while listening to heavy-metal rocker Ozzy Osbourne's "Suicide Solution" sued the singer. They argued that a low-noise hum on the record had a disturbing influence on the boy and made him lyrically pliable. The courts . . . dismissed the suit, giving First Amendment protection to the song. Thanks to the ruling, listeners are now responsible for their own behavior.

The Osbourne case was not the first time music has been said to cause suicide. There was a trend, of a sort, in "death rock" in the early '60s, epitomized by morbid teen songs like "Deadman's Curve" and "Last Kiss."

But before death rock came "Gloomy Sunday." According to David Ewen's *All the Years of American Popular Music*, the song was "promoted by its publishers as a 'suicide song' because it was reputed to have encouraged the suicidal tendencies of the tormented and the harassed of the early thirties." Written by Rezso Seress and translated by Sam M. Lewis, "Gloomy Sunday" was an import from equally gloomy Hungary. Billie Holiday recorded it in 1936 after it had been widely sung in concerts by Paul Robeson.

From that somber dirge of the Great Depression, America leaped into the "swing" era—and that too was roundly condemned. On October 25, 1938, the Archbishop of Dubuque, the Most Reverend Francis J.L. Beckman, labeled the swing music of Benny Goodman and others "a degenerate and demoralizing musical system" that had been "turned loose to gnaw away the moral fiber of young people." William E. Miles reports in *Damn It!* that the cleric told his flock that "jam sessions, jitterbugs and cannibalistic rhythmic orgies are wooing our youth along the primrose path to Hell!"

One of the most actively banned composers of the modern age was Cole Porter. From his first 1928 hits, "Let's Do It" and "Let's Misbehave," Porter's saucy lyrics have been deleted and banned with amazing consistency. "I get no kick from champagne" was originally "I get no kick from cocaine," but that was deemed too strong for the mass audience. "I'm a Gigolo," "You've Got That Thing," "My Heart Belongs to Daddy," and "Love for Sale" were often attacked and kept off the airwaves. . . .

Rock and Roll

When rock and roll burst upon the scene, it almost immediately became the censors' prime target. Elvis and his twitching, pumping pelvis; almost anything by the Rolling Stones; even the insipid "Puff, the Magic Dragon" by Peter, Paul, and Mary became the focus of conservative outrage.

"Puff," the 1963 flip side of "Blowin' in the Wind," was interpreted as a metaphorical celebration of pot smoking. As late as 1972 this was still a live issue—a radio station I worked for received angry letters when we played an *instrumental* version of the song. Ironically, ol' Puff is now a cartoon dragon seen on Saturday morning television.

Those who think that contemporary rock has gone "too far" along whatever personal highway to hell they're monitoring ought to look back 20 years—to the heyday of The Fugs. The name came from Norman Mailer's euphemism "Fug you" in *The Naked and the Dead*. Lillian Roxon's *Rock Encyclopedia* describes the group as "freaky-looking poets" from New York's East Village who "went out of their way to be 'offensive.'" She calls them "comics and satirists" and likens them to Lenny Bruce. It was, she notes, "like Henry Miller's novels set to music."

Feel the Beat

A lot of people have studied rock lyrics and they haven't been able to find any effects at all—no effects on socialization for instance. In one study, it was found that if you ask a high-school student to tell you the story of his favorite song, he can't. What they're listening to is the beat, just like they said on "American Bandstand."

Roger Desmond, quoted in *Socialist Review*, January/February 1986.

The Fugs's titles included: "Boobs a Lot," "Group Grope," "Dirty Old Man," "Kill for Peace," "New Amphet Amine Shriek," "I Command the House of the Devil," "Coca Cola Douche," "Wet Dream," "I Saw The Best Minds of My Generation Rot," and "Exorcising the Evil Spirits from the Pentagon." All prior to 1970.

It could probably be argued that Richard Nixon's Watergate exploits had a more disastrous influence on public ethics and morality in the '70 than did the music of The Fugs in the '60s or AC/DC in the '80s. And will be remembered longer.

"Satanic" Rock

Still, as Jimmy Swaggart's ministry has proven, some people will believe anything if it's screeched at them from a pulpit. In April 1986, according to the American Library Association's *Newsletter on Intellectual Freedom*, the Reverends Steven W. Timmons of Beloit, Wisconsin, and William A. Riedel, pastor of the Westwood United Pentecostal Church in Jackson, Michigan, spoke hell-raising sermons against "satanic" rock groups. Named as part of Lucifer's legion were such innocuous songsmiths as Abba, The Eagles, Stevie Nicks, and "probably the most powerful figure in this," John Denver.

Timmons told a flock of young people that "Rocky Mountain

High" teaches "witchcraft." (But wasn't it Sinatra who recorded "Witchcraft"? Or maybe it was "That Old Black Magic"? Or "That Old Devil Moon"?) The parishioners, worked up to a lather, buried a batch of rock records (and some Harlequin romance novels) under a tombstone that reads, "Never to rise again."

That same month, down in Ohio, a South Point evangelist named Jim Brown told his congregation that the theme song of TV's "Mr. Ed" contains hidden messages from Satan. He says he played the song backwards and heard, "the source is Satan." While singing "Oh, How I Love Jesus," the sappy psalmsters set about burning rock and country records and tapes. (If you want to check out the devil in Mr. Ed without rewiring your $1,200 Mitsubishi, use a reel-to-reel tape deck. Record the suspect song on the tape and then, without rewinding, take off the reels and place them on the opposite spindles. Then hit "Play.")

You hear what you listen for, of course. But it's a certainty that if it was possible to put backwards messages on records and have them subliminally influence forward-thinking listeners, people like Swaggart would be loading gospel records with injunctions to "Praise the Lord" and "Send the Money." . . .

Rowdy Songs?

Sample this lyric: "The havoc of war and the battle's confusion . . . their blood has washed out their foul footsteps' pollution." That's verse three; you might be more familiar with verse one, which includes: "And the rocket's red glare, the bombs bursting in air."

It's bad enough that our national anthem is set to the tune of a rowdy beer-drinking song—such a bad example for impressionable youth—but to encourage them to sing of such violent goings-on might inspire them to who-knows-what murderous actions!

It becomes obvious that if you really want to shield kids from sex and violence—from life itself—*everything* better have a warning label on it. And if music is going to be blamed for antisocial behavior, you'd better ban the Bible too. On August 22, 1986, an 18-year-old Miami high-school student named Alejandro Martinez stabbed his grandmother to death. He told police she interrupted him while he was reading the Bible and he thought she was the devil. For the well-being of the world's grandmothers, better prohibit sales of that book to minors. . . .

Narrow-Minded Censors

Lewd and obscene waltzes; scandalous ragtime and jazz; showtunes and blues red-penciled by bluenoses; Mr. Ed an agent of Satan; John Denver a warlock. Truly, it's a depressing catalog of narrow-minded boobery at work. Censors are people disturbed by what they perceive around them, who either don't understand the problem or who have manufactured a problem where none exists. They don't know what else to do but feel they have to do *something*. And censorship (no matter what other name they give it) of what they find offensive seems so quick, so easy. Out of sight, out of mind. You might just as well ban cars because some people drive drunk.

Hear No Evil

When I was a kid in the '60s, I grew up listening to rock 'n' roll songs. But there were others who attacked these songs because they thought rock 'n' roll music was going to destroy America's youth. They would show Elvis Presley "shakin'" only above the waist on television, and they would burn the records of the Beatles.

Well these censorship efforts were eventually turned back, and my generation turned out OK. But I've learned one valuable lesson about narrow-minded zealots: They never go away. . . .

There's nothing evil about today's rock 'n' roll. Elvis Costello is no more "a debilitating influence" in the '80s than Elvis Presley was in the '50s.

Anthony T. Podesta, *Houston Post*, October 16, 1986.

Calls for banning this or that seem to occur in cycles. There are clots of oversensitive, overreactive people in every generation, people resistant to and scared by change. Instead of thinking for themselves, they'll let their self-appointed leaders do it for them.

Thinking for yourself *is* dangerous. It carries with it the possibility of error as well as the weight of personal responsibility. For some people, that's too heavy a burden. They certainly have the right to denounce anything they don't like. But when they move to take what they don't like away from you, away from me, that's un-American. That's censorship.

"Television and film can . . . be used to enhance the comprehension and enjoyment of literature."

Television Should Be Used as a Teaching Aid

Patricia Marks Greenfield

Children spend more time watching television than they spend in the classroom. In an era of advancing electronic media, many educators want to keep pace with society by using television as a teaching tool. Patricia Marks Greenfield, a professor of psychology at UCLA, supports the use of television in the classroom. In the following viewpoint, Greenfield writes that TV can be used in conjunction with other media to provide a better learning experience for students.

As you read, consider the following questions:

1. What examples does the author give to prove TV's effectiveness in motivating students to read?
2. According to Greenfield, why does the transfer of skills from TV to print work so well?
3. In the author's opinion, why is a multimedia approach to education beneficial?

Many parents and teachers might worry that spending so much time on television in the classroom could further erode reading and writing skills. However, the electronic media can also be used in schools to help build print literacy. . . .

Television and film can . . . be used to enhance the comprehension and enjoyment of literature, especially on the part of the less able students. Working with junior high school students, Elias Levinson looked at how their response to short stories (by authors such as O. Henry) differed depending on the medium of presentation. One group of students read the original story; another group both read the story and saw it on film. Levinson investigated their comprehension (including recall) and enjoyment (assessed by the desire to read more stories of the same type). Overall, he found that the addition of the film very much increased comprehension and enjoyment, especially for students with lower IQ's. The advantage added by the film was also greater for the more unfamiliar stories, indicating that film or television could be particularly valuable for unfamiliar subjects or genres.

It is interesting that the films stimulated not only comprehension and memory of the story but also a desire to read more similar stories. It is also important that the effect of film on reading is greatest for the children who tend to have more problems in school, that is, the low-IQ group. This study demonstrates the potential for using television to enhance reading. Contrary to popular opinion, books and television need not be two media at war with each other.

Indeed, movies tend to make certain books popular with children. A survey of sixth, seventh, and eighth graders in New Jersey showed that 40 percent of the books they chose to read were tied to television or movies. In England in the 1950s it was found that both television and radio dramatizations, some serialized, caused many children to read the dramatized books, many of which were classics.

TV as a Motivator

Some teachers are beginning to take advantage of television's ability to motivate reading. A flavor of the rather dramatic results that can be obtained is conveyed by Rosemary Lee Potter, a pioneer in the use of out-of-school television in school:

> One day a sixth-grader named Clara came in with a paperback copy of *The Little House on the Prairie*. Clara was not a great reader. I had never seen her with an unassigned book. It was quite a surprise for me to see her bring in a rather thickish book and read it. No doubt noticing my surprise, she quickly explained to me that *she had seen it on TV!* . . . I scoured book shelves, libraries, and booklists . . . I found a bounty of television-related books for my students . . . I began to bring these books into the classroom. Students showed high interest. Most of the books

soon fell apart with excessive wear. Students who had previously been nonreaders read everything from the latest about Fonzie to well-known books like *Sounder*.

Another way of using television in the schools, one that has become increasingly common in the United States in recent years, is to read television scripts in the classroom. The television networks now release their scripts in advance; CBS distributes millions of scripts and coordinated teacher's guides each year. There is an organization, Capital Cities Television Reading Program, that distributes advance scripts, along with coordinated teacher's guides and student workbooks. Teachers in Philadelphia who used scripts from television programs reported improved reading scores and much more interest in reading. Scripts were even stolen from the classroom, the first known theft of reading material in that school.

Better Prepared

The fact is that television . . . has plodded on with results, at least to children, that are a far cry from the warnings sounded. . . . Study after study shows that school children today come better prepared to learn, and more informed, as a result of television, than any generation before.

Dorothy Rabinowitz, *The Washington Times*, January 26, 1987.

Television shows and films can also be treated as literature in school. Sharon Neuwirth, a fourth grade teacher, noticed that her children were retelling their favorite television shows in class in great detail, but that they were totally oblivious to the story line. (Her observation agrees with the experimental research on the subject.) She noticed the same tendency to focus on peripheral detail in discussing stories read in class and in book reports. To counteract this, Neuwirth developed a project to teach story comprehension, focusing on conflict as the key to a story's structure:

> I explained to the students that a conflict is set up when a character has a problem to solve: he wants or needs something, but an obstacle stands in his way. For example, a new student wants to make friends, but he's shy. Or a teacher is determined to help a student who wants to drop out of school. . .
>
> To tune the students into looking for the basic conflict, I gave them an unusual homework assignment: watch anything you like on TV, and be prepared tomorrow to tell about your show in only three sentences—Who the show was about, what the main character wanted, and what stood in his or her way.

From this assignment, Neuwirth had the class branch off into identifying conflict in other media: film, school plays, and short stories. One effect of learning to understand the basic structure of a story was that the children could, for the first time, read long novels. They had been unable to do so before because, lacking a sense of overall structure, they were simply overwhelmed by complex plots.

Neuwirth's project succeeded because she began with television. The medium was available to all the children, no matter what their reading level, and they were already highly motivated to watch and discuss televison shows. Once concepts were learned in relation to this familiar medium, they could be transferred to more difficult and less familiar ones, notably print. Surely this program will make children more sophisticated and comprehending viewers, as well as making them better readers.

Level of Expertise

One reason why the transfer of skills from television to print works so well may be that children start at a higher level of expertise in the former medium. In England, Michael Scarborough has investigated the educational use of entertainment television with ten and eleven-year-old children, and has come to the following conclusions:

> Perhaps the most significant outcome to emerge from this effort was the considerable depth and sophistication in the child's conceptualization. Certainly they more readily articulated their understanding of programmes than they might have done had the exercise been based on written material of comparable content and difficulty. It might be that this is an indication of the child's intelligence and scholastic achievement, from my work it is impossible to say clearly if this is so, but my opinion is that because there is a widespread familiarity with the medium of television, children of a wide range of abilities are at ease in expressing their understanding of what they have viewed.

These classroom techniques could all be interpreted as showing the value of multimedia education: in each case, television or film is an addition to print, not a substitute for it. Indeed, one of the most consistent findings in the literature on media in education is the superiority of multimedia over single-medium presentation. In fact, in talking about media in schools, one is always talking about adding media to the original medium of face-to-face interaction with the teacher. And face-to-face interaction adds as much to the learning value of any medium as the medium adds to the classroom.

Value of Multimedia Education

There are various reasons why it should be of value to have the same material presented through more than one medium. Each medium, because of its code of representation and its technical capabilities, must emphasize different kinds of information. For example, film or television emphasizes action and simultaneous events happening in parallel. Print, in contrast, emphasizes a linear, sequential relationship between ideas or events. Thus, to receive information on the same topic through different media is to learn about the topic from different points of view.

Our present educational system is so print-oriented that we tend to think of an account in print as the "true" one. In education, print is truly a privileged medium of communication. This is probably mainly a result of historical circumstance: print was there first. It is time to question this assumption, not thinking of replacing print, but of moving from domination by a single medium to an increasingly multimedia system.

"The television style of learning . . . is, by its nature, hostile to what has been called book-learning, or, its handmaiden, school-learning."

Television Should Not Be Used as a Teaching Aid

Neil Postman

Television was once described as a "vast wasteland." With the emergence of educational children's programs some of the negative publicity over TV lessened. Neil Postman, a professor of communication arts and sciences at New York University, thinks that educators should remain wary of mass media. In the following viewpoint, Postman argues that using television in the classroom would make education mere entertainment.

As you read, consider the following questions:

1. Why does the author believe *Sesame Street* undermines the traditional idea of schooling?
2. In Postman's opinion, what has been television's main contribution to educational philosophy?
3. Why does he think the three commandments of TV detract from education?

There could not have been a safer bet when it began in 1969 than that "Sesame Street" would be embraced by children, parents and educators. Children loved it because they were raised on television commercials, which they intuitively knew were the most carefully crafted entertainments on television. To those who had not yet been to school, even to those who had just started, the idea of being *taught* by a series of commercials did not seem peculiar. And that television should entertain them was taken as a matter of course.

Parents embraced "Sesame Street" for several reasons, among them that it assuaged their guilt over the fact that they could not or would not restrict their children's access to television. "Sesame Street" appeared to justify allowing a four- or five-year-old to sit transfixed in front of a television screen for unnatural periods of time. Parents were eager to hope that television could teach their children something other than which breakfast cereal has the most crackle. At the same time, "Sesame Street" relieved them of the responsibility of teaching their pre-school children how to read— no small matter in a culture where children are apt to be considered a nuisance. They could also plainly see that in spite of its faults, "Sesame Street" was entirely consonant with the prevailing spirit of America. Its use of cute puppets, celebrities, catchy tunes, and rapid-fire editing was certain to give pleasure to the children and would therefore serve as adequate preparation for their entry into a fun-loving culture.

As for educators, they generally approved of "Sesame Street," too. Contrary to common opinion, they are apt to find new methods congenial, especially if they are told that education can be accomplished more efficiently by means of the new techniques. (That is why such ideas as "teacher-proof" textbooks, standardized tests, and, now, micro-computers have been welcomed into the classroom.) "Sesame Street" appeared to be an imaginative aid in solving the growing problem of teaching Americans how to read, while, at the same time, encouraging children to love school.

Undermining Influence

We now know that "Sesame Street" encourages children to love school only if school is like "Sesame Street." Which is to say, we now know that "Sesame Street" undermines what the traditional idea of schooling represents. Whereas a classroom is a place of social interaction, the space in front of a television set is a private preserve. Whereas in a classroom, one may ask a teacher questions, one can ask nothing of a television screen. Whereas school is centered on the development of language, television demands attention to images. Whereas attending school is a legal requirement, watching television is an act of choice. Whereas in school, one fails to attend to the teacher at the risk of punishment, no

SPEAKING OF
T.V. SCRAMBLING...

Steve Kelley, reprinted with permission.

penalties exist for failing to attend to the television screen. Whereas to behave oneself in school means to observe rules of public decorum, television watching requires no such observances, has no concept of public decorum. Whereas in a classroom, fun is never more than a means to an end, on television it is the end in itself.

Yet "Sesame Street" and its progeny, "The Electric Company," are not to be blamed for laughing the traditional classroom out of existence. If the classroom now begins to seem a stale and flat environment for learning, the inventors of television itself are to blame, not the Children's Television Workshop. We can hardly expect those who want to make good television shows to concern themselves with what the classroom is for. They are concerned with what television is for. This does not mean that "Sesame Street" is not educational. It is, in fact, nothing but educational—in the sense that every television show is educational. Just as reading a book—any kind of book—promotes a particular orientation toward learning, watching a television show does the same. "The Little House on the Prairie," "Cheers" and "The Tonight Show" are as effective as "Sesame Street" in promoting what might be called the television style of learning. And this style of learning is, by its nature, hostile to what has been called book-learning or its handmaiden, school-learning. If we are to blame "Sesame Street" for anything, it is for the pretense that it is any ally of the classroom. That, after all, has been its chief claim on foundation and public money. As a television show, and a good one, "Sesame Street" does not encourage children to love school or anything about school. It encourages them to love television.

Learning How To Learn

Moreover, it is important to add that whether or not "Sesame Street" teaches children their letters and numbers is entirely irrelevant. We may take as our guide here John Dewey's observation that the content of a lesson is the least important thing about learning. As he wrote in *Experience and Education:* "Perhaps the greatest of all pedagogical fallacies is the notion that a person learns only what he is studying at the time. Collateral learning in the way of formation of enduring attitudes . . . may be and often is more important than the spelling lesson or lesson in geography or history. . . . For these attitudes are fundamentally what count in the future." In other words, the most important thing one learns is always about *how* one learns. . . .

Television's principal contribution to educational philosophy is the idea that teaching and entertainment are inseparable. This entirely original conception is to be found nowhere in educational discourses, from Confucius to Plato to Cicero to Locke to John Dewey. In searching the literature of education, you will find it said by some that children will learn best when they are interested in what they are learning. You will find it said—Plato and Dewey emphasized this—that reason is best cultivated when it is rooted in robust emotional ground. You will even find some who say that learning is best facilitated by a loving and benign teacher. But no one has ever said or implied that significant learning is effectively, durably and truthfully achieved when education is entertainment. Education philosophers have assumed that becoming acculturated is difficult because it necessarily involves the imposition of restraints. They have argued that there must be a sequence to learning, that perseverance and a certain measure of perspiration are indispensable, that individual pleasures must frequently be submerged in the interests of group cohesion, and that learning to be critical and to think conceptually and rigorously do not come easily to the young but are hard-fought victories. Indeed, Cicero remarked that the purpose of education is to free the student from the tyranny of the present, which cannot be pleasurable for those, like the young, who are struggling hard to do the opposite—that is, accommodate themselves to the present.

Television offers a delicious and, as I have said, original alternative to all of this. We might say there are three commandments that form the philosophy of the education which television offers. The influence of these commandments is observable in every type

142

of television programming—from "Sesame Street" to the documentaries of "Nova" and "The National Geographic" to "Fantasy Island" to MTV. The commandments are as follows:

Thou shalt have no prerequisites

Every television program must be a complete package in itself. No previous knowledge is to be required. There must not be even a hint that learning is hierarchical, that it is an edifice constructed on a foundation. The learner must be allowed to enter at any point without prejudice. This is why you shall never hear or see a television program begin with the caution that if the viewer has not seen the previous programs, this one will be meaningless. Television is a nongraded curriculum and excludes no viewer for any reason, at any time. In other words, in doing away with the idea of sequence and continuity in education, television undermines the idea that sequence and continuity have anything to do with thought itself.

Thou shalt induce no perplexity

In television teaching, perplexity is a superhighway to low ratings. A perplexed learner is a learner who will turn to another station. This means that there must be nothing that has to be remembered, studied, applied or, worst of all, endured. It is assumed that any information, story or idea can be made immediately accessible, since the contentment, not the growth, of the learner is paramount.

Thou shalt avoid exposition like the ten plagues visited upon Egypt

Of all the enemies of television-teaching, including continuity and perplexity, none is more formidable than exposition. Arguments, hypotheses, discussions, reasons, refutations or any of the traditional instruments of reasoned discourse turn television into radio or, worse, third-rate printed matter. Thus, television-teaching always takes the form of story-telling, conducted through dynamic images and supported by music. This is as characteristic of "Star Trek" as it is of "Cosmos," of "Diff'rent Strokes" as of "Sesame Street," of commercials as of "Nova." Nothing will be taught on television that cannot be both visualized and placed in a theatrical context.

The name we may properly give to an education without prerequisites, perplexity and exposition is entertainment. And when one considers that save for sleeping there is no activity that occupies more of an American youth's time than television-viewing, we cannot avoid the conclusion that a massive reorientation toward learning is now taking place. . . . The consequences of this reorientation are to be observed not only in the decline of the potency of the classroom but, paradoxically, in the refashioning of the classroom into a place where both teaching and learning are intended to be vastly amusing activities.

Recognizing Statements That Are Provable

From various sources of information we are constantly confronted with statements and generalizations about social and political issues. This is especially true when dealing with subjects in which statistical research is difficult, such as the media's influence on society. In order to think clearly about these subjects, it is useful if one can make a distinction between statements for which evidence can be found and other statements which cannot be verified because evidence is not available, or because the issue is so controversial that it cannot be definitely proved.

Readers should constantly be aware that magazines, newspapers, and other sources often contain statements of a controversial nature. The following activity is designed to strengthen readers' ability to recognize statements that are provable and those that are not.

Most of the following statements are taken from the viewpoints in this chapter. Consider each statement carefully. *Mark P for any statement you believe is provable. Mark U for any statement you think is unprovable because of the lack of evidence. Mark C for statements you find too controversial to be proved to everyone's satisfaction.*

If you are doing this activity as a member of a class or group, compare your answers with those of other class or group members. Be able to defend your answers. You may discover that others will come to different conclusions than you. Listening to the reasons others present for their answers may give you valuable insights in recognizing statements that are provable.

P = *provable*
U = *unprovable*
C = *too controversial*

1. The minute Japan bombed Pearl Harbor, the media launched a national defense campaign and whipped American patriotic spirit into such a frenzy that we attacked both Japan and Germany.

2. The media moguls wield immense power, yet this power is being used to destroy our culture, concepts of right and wrong and family ties.

3. The effect of films on reading abilities is greatest for the children who have more problems in school, that is, the low-IQ group.

4. People are not readily used by the media.

5. In various direct and indirect ways, the public acts upon the mass media rather than simply being influenced by them.

6. Vietnam stands as a national disgrace, not because we could not win, but because the media so intimidated our national leaders that they would not let us win.

7. In England in the 1950s, it was found that both television and radio dramatizations caused children to read dramatized books, many of which were classics.

8. The electronic media can be used in schools to help build print literacy.

9. We know that *Sesame Street* undermines the traditional idea of education.

10. Educational television does not teach children to love school, it teaches them to love television.

11. There is no activity that occupies more of an American youth's time, save for sleeping, than television viewing.

12. The record companies and rock stars know exactly what effect music has on young people. They know they are encouraging young people to commit suicide.

13. Violent videos can have harmful effects on their young viewers. There is a desensitizing of individuals who watch violent videos.

14. It could be argued that Richard Nixon's Watergate had a more disastrous influence on public ethics and morality in the '70s than did the music of the Fugs in the '60s or AC/DC in the '80s.

Periodical Bibliography

The following articles have been selected to supplement the diverse views expressed in this chapter.

William F. Fore — "Media Violence: Hazardous to Our Health," *The Christian Century*, September 25, 1985.

Randy Frame — "Violence for Fun," *Christianity Today*, February 21, 1986.

Todd Gitlin — "The Lone Driver Rides Again," *The Progressive*, February 1987.

Meg Greenfield — "The Media Made Me Do It," *Newsweek*, April 7, 1986.

Nat Hentoff — "The Disc Washers," *The Progressive*, November 1985.

B.H. Joffe — "Commercial Television Can Be Used for Teaching," *Education Digest*, October 1986.

John Leland — "Don't Knock Shock Rock," *High Times*, January 1986.

Media and Values — "Rock and Its Role," Winter 1986.

Gerald Nachman — "Rock and a Hard Place," *The New American*, February 17, 1986.

Newsweek — "So Who Understands Rock Lyrics Anyway?" July 14, 1986.

Parents' Music Resource Center [PMRC] — *The Record.* Any issue. Available from 1500 Arlington Blvd., Arlington, VA 22209.

Michael J. Robinson — "An Absence of Malice: Young People and the Press," *Public Opinion*, November/December 1986.

Joe Saltzman — "Porn Rock," *USA Today*, January 1986.

Jay W. Stein — "Shotgun Wedding: Television and the Schools," *USA Today*, November 1983.

U.S. News & World Report — "Censor Entertainment? Teens, Parents Speak Up," October 28, 1985.

How Do the Media Affect Politics?

Chapter Preface

Many political analysts believe the media wield too much power over America's governmental processes. Others think politicians have too much power over the media, using these sources of public information to promote their political ambitions. The question of who controls whom is important when analyzing the media's role in politics.

The media's critics theorize that certain candidates become media favorites. During an election, they contend, journalists highlight not the candidates with the most political savvy, but those who are exciting on camera or in print. These critics cite the example of the grade B film actor, Ronald Reagan, who became California's governor and then president of the United States, largely because of his media appeal.

Others say that politicians skillfully manipulate the media to gain votes and political power. Politicians, they argue, understand the media and use journalists to their advantage. What else could explain the hiring of campaign managers who specialize in grooming their candidates to sound and look good to media audiences?

The viewpoints in this chapter debate the impact of the media on elections as well as other issues reflecting the nature of the media's political influence.

"The media now weigh so heavily on the scales of power that . . . we are upsetting the historic checks and balances invented by our forefathers."

The Media Influence Politics

Michael J. O'Neill

The mass media have become America's primary source of information in the political process. Cable television covers US Congress sessions. Presidents address the nation on network television. Public criticism of elected officials takes place in newspapers and magazines. Supporters of the media believe this extensive coverage of politics generates healthy debate. Detractors think the coverage hinders America's federal policymaking. In the following viewpoint, Michael J. O'Neill, former editor of the *New York Daily News*, writes that the media have become too powerful. O'Neill argues that the media have a negative effect on federal policymaking by giving priority to certain political issues while overlooking others.

As you read, consider the following questions:

1. What danger does the author see in the media becoming too powerful?
2. According to the author, how do the media influence certain political issues prematurely?
3. In O'Neill's opinion, why is media accountability necessary?

Michael J. O'Neill, "The Power of the Press," a presidential address to the American Society of Newspaper Editors, 1982. Reprinted with permission from the *Proceedings* of the American Society of Newspaper Editors and the author.

The extraordinary powers of the media, most convincingly displayed by network television and the national press, have been mobilized to influence major public issues and national elections, to help diffuse the authority of Congress and to disassemble the political parties—even to make Presidents or to break them. Indeed, the media now weigh so heavily on the scales of power that some political scientists claim we are upsetting the historic checks and balances invented by our forefathers. Samuel P. Huntington of Harvard has observed that "during the '60's and '70's, the media were the institution whose power expanded most significantly and that posed the most serious challenges to governmental authority." Max M. Kampelman has similarly warned that "the relatively unrestrained power of the media may well represent an even greater challenge to democracy than the much publicized abuses of power by the Executive and the Congress." And Sen. Daniel P. Moynihan, who concedes the press already has the upper hand in Washington, says that if the balance should tip too far in its direction "our capacity for effective democratic government will be seriously and dangerously weakened."

This is flattering, of course, because all newspapermen dream of being movers and shakers and the thought that we may actually be threatening the national government is inspirational. In several respects, it is also true. The Communications Revolution, which is profoundly reshaping all of Western society, has also altered the basic terms of reference between the press and American democracy.

More than Messengers

No longer are we just the messengers, observers on the sidelines, witch's mirrors faithfully telling society how it looks. Now we are deeply imbedded in the democratic process itself, as principal actors rather than bit players or mere audience.

No longer do we merely cover the news. Thanks mainly to television, we are often partners now in the creation of news—unwilling and unwitting partners, perhaps, but partners nonetheless in producing what Daniel Boorstin has deplored as pseudoevents, pseudoprotests, pseudocrises and controversies.

No longer do we look on government only with the healthy skepticism required by professional tradition. Now we have a hard, intensely adversarial attitude. We treat the government as the enemy—and government officials as convenient targets for attack-and-destroy missions.

No longer do we submit automatically to the rigors of old-fashioned impartiality. Now, not always but too often, we surrender to the impulse of advocacy, in the name of reform but forgetful of balance, fairness and—if it isn't too unfashionable to say so—what is good for the country.

150

These trends, however, are more symptom than cause. Much deeper processes are at work. The mass media, especially television, are not only changing the way government is covered but the way it functions. The crucial relationship between the people and their elected representatives—the very core of our political system—has been altered fundamentally.

In ways that Jefferson and Hamilton never intended nor could even imagine, Americans now have the whole world delivered to them every day, in pulsating, living color—all of life swept inside their personal horizon. Distant events—Selma, Alabama ... the riot-torn Democratic convention in Chicago ... the hostages in Iran—are instant experiences, neither insulated by a reporter's translation nor muted by what Theodore H. White has called the consoling "filter of time."

The flashing images mobilize popular emotions on a truly massive scale and with stunning speed, quickly generating and shaping public opinion. The televised battle scenes from Vietnam, as we know, aroused a whole nation against the war, helped reverse our national policy and ultimately destroyed the presidency of Lyndon Johnson.

The Agenda Setters

Political issues do not just "happen." Creating an issue, dramatizing it, calling attention to it, and pressuring government to do something about it are important political tactics. These are the tactics of agenda setting. They are employed by influential persons, organized interest groups, political candidates, government leaders, and, most importantly, the mass media themselves.

Thomas R. Dye and L. Harmon Zeigler, *American Politics in the Media Age*, 1983.

"The introduction of modern mass communications," said the sociologist Daniel Bell, "allows us, in many cases forces us, to respond directly and immediately to social issues." Television has thus played a decisive role in the so-called revolution of rising expectations. It has strongly stimulated the consumption culture. It has dramatized the gap between haves and have nots, helping to create a runaway demand for more and more government services and for equality of result as well as of opportunity.

Forcing the Issues

Time and time again, Presidents discover that the public has already made up its mind about issues before they have even had time to consider them. Their hand is forced. The deliberative process that representative government was designed to assure is frustrated.

Television has also indelibly changed the democratic process by establishing a direct communication link between political leaders and their constituents. Now, as never before, these politicians are able to bypass the print media and the troublesome business of depending on reporters to represent them to the public.

More significant, but for the same reason, they are also able to bypass their parties so that the whole system of party government, built up over nearly two centuries, is now breaking down. This, in turn, is contributing to the crisis of government that Lloyd Cutler and others find so threatening to the American system. . . .

Damaging the Process

If the credibility of news coverage has been hurt, the functioning of government has been damaged even more. Not only are public issues and priorities strongly influenced by the media, every policy initiative, every action, has to run a gauntlet of criticism that is often generated—and always amplified—by the press. In the searing glare of daily coverage, an official's every personal flaw, every act, every mistake, every slip of the tongue, every display of temper is recorded, magnified and ground into the public consciousness.

The protests of special-interest groups, the charges of publicity-hungry congressmen, are rock-and-rolled through the halls of power. Controversy and conflict are sought out wherever they can be found, sapping energies and usually diverting attention from more urgent public business.

In this whirling centrifuge of criticism and controversy, authority is dissipated. Officials are undermined and demoralized. The capacity to govern, already drastically reduced by the fragmentation of power, is weakened still further. . . .

Television in a Political World

The problem of television is formidable. Its baleful effect on both government and journalism is beyond repeal. The expanding network news shows and the proliferation of cable promise even more change, confusion and competition for the attention of busy Americans. And there are no solutions that I can think of, only the possibility of limited damage control. The key to this is to emphasize the basics, the things newspapers have always been able to do better than television, services that will become even more important as the electronic networks continue swarming over the mass market and, in the process, define a more specialized role for newspapers.

We should be more resistant than ever to media hype—the pseudoevent, the phoney charges, the staged protest, the packaged candidate, the prime-time announcement and televised interview. Indeed, we should expose these as vigorously as we expose official corruption. For it is our job to cut through the superficial

152

to identify the substantive—to explain and clarify the news, as most newspapers already do, in a reasoned way that television cannot. Although we should be interesting, we should not try to be an entertainment like television, because this would be both futile and out of keeping with our special purpose.

Accountable and Self Disciplined

Another issue is accountability. A brooding Ray Price, formerly of the New York Herald Tribune and the White House, complained that the press had acquired power "out of all proportion" to its ability or inclination to use it responsibly. Walter Wriston, a banker speaking for many in public life, warned that the media should remember that "the effective functioning of a democracy requires the most difficult of all disciplines, self-discipline."

"The freedom of us all," he said, "rides with the freedom of the press. Nevertheless, its continued freedom and ours will ultimately depend upon the media not exploiting to the fullest their unlimited power."

"What Congress is doing at any one time is determined by many factors not directly influenced by the press."

The Media Do Not Influence Politics

Stephen Hess

Candidates on the campaign trail must face a barrage of media coverage. Journalists confront politicians about their inconsistencies and failed promises. Editorials often publicize controversial issues many officials in government would rather ignore. Yet, despite the media's focus on government, some analysts do not believe the media unduly influence American politics. Stephen Hess, a senior fellow at the Brookings Institution, spent a year in Washington observing the relationship between Congress members and the media. In the following viewpoint, Hess argues that the media only react to political processes, they do not influence them.

As you read, consider the following questions:

1. In the author's opinion, why aren't political officials affected by their heavy news consumption?
2. According to Hess, why don't most politicians use the media to influence legislation?
3. How does Hess explain the media's reputation for influencing politics?

Stephen Hess, *The Ultimate Insiders: U.S. Senators in the National Media*. Washington, DC: Brookings Books, 1986. Reprinted with permission.

There is no shortage of claims for the power of the press on Capitol Hill. Starting with the classic study by Donald Matthews in 1960, scholars and others seem to agree that "reporters play an important role in the operation of the Senate and profoundly shape the behavior of its members." More recently, Joel Havemann of the *Los Angeles Times* wrote that "a complex but symbiotic relationship has developed between Congress and the news media. It is a relationship that begins in the self-interest of both, yet ultimately helps shape everything from next year's election returns to the most far-reaching of public policy decisions." So many knowledgeable people, including senators, tell us that this is so that surely it must be so.

The most obvious reason why influence is attributed to the media is that the members of Congress, and especially their staffs, are incorrigible news junkies. Michael J. Robinson and Maura E. Clancey have quantified this phenomenon. "The average senior [congressional] staff member claims to spend almost two and a half hours per day watching, reading or listening to these national news media," they wrote in *Washington Journalism Review*. As I wandered through Senator Moynihan's offices at 8:45 on a January morning, the scene reminded me of those cartoon ads for the old *Philadelphia Bulletin* ("nearly everyone in Philadelphia reads the *Bulletin*"): the senator's administrative assistant, personal secretary, press secretary, assistant press secretary, and office manager were all hidden behind a morning newspaper. Heavy consumption may not be bad for one's health, but it seems logical to assume that it will have an effect.

No Cause and Effect

The problem is that cause and effect are so difficult to match up. One of the few times that the connection has been certain came in early 1977 when the *Washington Post*, the newspaper with the largest readership on Capitol Hill, assigned reporter T.R. Reid to follow week by week a little-known piece of legislation through Congress. The *Post*'s editors chose a perennial loser called the "waterway user charge bill" (it would require those who ship freight on the nation's canals and rivers to help the government pay for waterway maintenance). This time the bill passed. Its chief Senate sponsor, Pete Domenici, told Reid, "You know, there's probably 500 good policy ideas floating around on the Hill at any one time, but most of them just aren't getting on the front page of the *Post* every week."

During the year I spent as an observer at the Senate. I did not see any cause and effect. I saw a lot of reporters writing stories. I saw a lot of bills being voted up or down. The stories often helped explain the votes, but I do not think the stories caused the votes. Yet it was a year in which the lawyer for the attorney general-designate accused Senator Howard Metzenbaum of "systematically leaking" material to the press that was "inflammatory" and "extremely prejudicial" to his client; a year in which a private investigator admitted taping conversations in which a member of the Senate Labor Committee staff was leaking information to columnist Jack Anderson about the committee's investigation of the secretary of labor; a year in which Senators Barry Goldwater and Daniel P. Moynihan jointly rebuked Senator Jesse Helms for disclosing information from the Senate Intelligence Committee, a charge that Helms vehemently denied. Obviously there were interactions between senators (or their surrogates) and journalists that were intended to be (as Havemann puts it) "in the self-interest of both." Still, they caused remarkably few ripples that could be said to have nudged public policy questions in a manner that might not have happened had they not been reported in the national media. . . .

Widespread Ignorance

The power of the media . . . has been exaggerated. There are a number of constraints and limitations of the ability of the media to persuade and inform. Perhaps the most ironic and persistent thorn in the side of the theory of powerful media effects is the repeated demonstration of widespread political ignorance despite the plentiful opportunities for exposure to political information in the media.

W. Russell Neuman, *The Paradox of Mass Politics*, 1986.

Joseph Califano, who has watched Congress from an executive-branch perspective, has noted, "Look at the *Congressional Record* in the House on any significant debate and you can find 50 good quotes because they're all fighting to be one of those guys who gets into the [Dan] Rather coverage." Since we now know that members of Congress hardly ever make the CBS evening news unless they are running for president or hold leadership positions, this could be described as a catalytic effect—the media changing the behavior of Congress without actually entering the process itself. The importance of the national media, then, would be not what it reports (and can be held accountable for), but simply that it is there; not what gets on the air or in print, but what members of Congress try to get on the air or in print. We should not discount the effect of the media just because we cannot measure it. (But neither should we accept its influence solely on the basis of intuitive reasoning.) In fact, in Califano's example what the members of the House are doing in the "50 good quotes" is primarily trying to get their local TV and radio stations to show them in action from the House floor. They are often successful, and Dan Rather does not have much to do with their behavior.

Because most senators (and House members) get almost no attention in the national media, it is not necessary for them to engage the national press corps in their legislative strategies. If they want to get a bill passed—to get from here to there in the legislative process—they rarely make the journey by mobilizing the press. Trying to use the media to get legislation through Congress is a Rube Goldberg design based on (A) legislator influencing (B) reporter to get information into (C) news outlet so as to convince (D) voters who will then put pressure on (E) other legislators. Given all of the problems inherent in successfully maneuvering through the maze, no wonder that legislative strategies are usually variations of (A) legislator asking (E) other legislators for their support through personal conversation, "Dear Colleague" letters, caucuses, or other means. Of course, some legislators, acting out of optimism or ignorance or arrogance, may choose to use the media even though it is a highly inefficient legislative strategy.

Occasionally I saw a senator call a press conference for what I felt was a pedagogical purpose, trying to educate reporters to the importance or intricacies of an issue. Generally, however, most of the press relations that I watched in 1984 involved the three activities that David Mayhew concluded are "electorally useful [for legislators] to engage in"—advertising, credit claiming, and position taking—that is, trying to create a favorable image with messages that have little content, showing that pleasing things happen because voters had the wisdom to elect a particular legislator, and making judgmental statements that are expected to agree with the views of certain constituencies. . . .

Blatant Messages

There is some signaling through the media by Senate leaders who wish to send messages to the White House. But they are so blatant, says the *Post*'s Helen Dewar, that reporters know how to assess their intentions. In the year that I watched the majority leader's press secretary, Tommy Griscom, in his Capitol alcove briefings for the congressional press corps, he never resorted to the type of cuing that is a ritual at the White House and State Department, where "I can't confirm or deny" may mean "It's true, but I won't say that on the record." When Griscom was asked to assess the chances of Baker's pet project (a bill to televise the Senate proceedings), which we all knew was doomed to defeat, he replied, "Paul, don't ask. I haven't lied to you in four years, and I'm not going to start now."

Also, it is not necessary for senators to use the press as an internal means of communication. Officials of the State Department and the Pentagon have remarkably few opportunities to interact with one another, but each reads what the other is thinking as reported in the pages of the *Washington Post* and *New York Times* (papers that are widely circulated throughout agencies by means of press clipping services). Senators do not need reporters to speak for them because Capitol Hill is a very small enclave, physically and socially. During the fight over who would succeed Howard Baker as Republican leader, for example, I asked Bob Packwood if competing senators were using leaks and columns like "Washington Whispers" [in U.S. *News & World Report*]. He replied, "That would be a dangerous game. There are only fifty-four of us." (In fact, one contender for the leadership post later appeared in "Washington Whispers" in what had all the signs of a press secretary's plant. The senator was badly defeated, although again there is no way of knowing whether the story contributed to the outcome.). . .

Poor Recall

To a large extent, only the political elite attend to the political press. For every household that receives a journal of political opinion such as the *New Republic* or *National Review*, there are 100 households that subscribe to *Good Housekeeping* and 400 that subscribe to *TV Guide*. . . .

Even when the audience does run across some political content amid the media flow, there are further barriers to communication. Despite the average level of media exposure in a given day, which probably involves over four hours of television as well as exposure to newspapers and magazines, citizens remember little of what they see and read.

W. Russell Neuman, *The Paradox of Mass Politics*, 1986.

The notion that journalists impose upon Congress their view of what is significant—as some scholars contend—is not the impression I brought back from my observations. What Congress is doing at any one time is determined by many factors not directly influenced by the press—the inflation rate, the unemployment rate, the crime rate, what the president asks the Congress to do, controversial decisions of the Supreme Court, acts of terrorists, acts of nature. The order of business is set by the majority leader, the ultimate insider, after consultation with his committee chairmen. What is then reported in the national media is largely a reflection of this process. The popular judgment of journalism researchers that "the press does not tell the people what to think, it tells the people what to think about" is simply not the case on Capitol Hill. This press corps is almost totally reactive.

National reporters also may become less influential on Capitol

Hill as additional sources of information become available to the legislators and their assistants. Writing about the role of the press in the Israeli legislature, for instance, Dorit Phyllis Gary concludes, "since Knesset members do not enjoy large staffs, most of the legislative queries and motions are based on media reports. . . . " But U.S. senators and members of the House of Representatives now have very large staffs, and they produce for their employers a type of tailor-made material that suits specific legislative and political needs. One step removed from the research designed for legislators' personal needs are the large committee staffs that service their party needs and ideological needs. Various sorts of computerized services, just now coming to the Senate, will give staffs even more information that is not dependent on the news media. While the local media provide vital information about state or district affairs, events covered in the national media are rarely actionable, even though they may be important and interesting. Legislators listening to the network news are mostly like the rest of us, shaking our heads over the sad state of affairs in Chad or Centralia.

There are, however, certain specialized publications that retain their influence because they are precise enough to help legislators and their assistants in their work. A member of the Senate Finance Committee staff, for example, might subscribe to *Daily Tax Report* or *Tax Notes*, a weekly magazine. Probably every office relies on *Congressional Quarterly*. Sitting at a table reserved for the press in a Capitol dining room in August 1984, Dale Tale of *Congressional Quarterly* told me, "Most stories [by other reporters] today will say, 'The Senate is tied up in procedural knots,' and then move on. But I will have to write a story about the procedural knots."

A Nonexistent Power

Ultimately, a lot more people and groups have an interest in noting the power of the press than in showing that media power sometimes may be akin to that of the Wizard of Oz. There is, of course, the press itself. As Hedley Donovan, the former editor in chief of *Time*, observed with regard to President Kennedy, "We loved being read so closely." There are also certain participants in the governmental process who must find it useful to blame "media power" for their own failures or frustrations. Books about the power that is will always sell better than those about the power that is not. And finally, there are media researchers whose entitlements in the world of conference going and journal articles— regardless of whether we are praising, pointing with alarm, or remaining truly neutral—will be in direct proportion to our colleagues' sense that we are writing about one of the real power players in public policy. This then becomes a collective bias of which readers should be aware. Beware.

159

"Being 'good on television' has become one of the first requirements for being a successful candidate."

The Media Have Great Impact on US Elections

Austin Ranney

During the 1960 presidential election campaign John F. Kennedy scored a media triumph in a televised debate with Richard M. Nixon. While the handsome Kennedy appeared to be comfortable in front of the cameras, Nixon seemed ill-at-ease and nervous. Many political scientists believe that debate spawned the television age in politics. In the following viewpoint, Austin Ranney, a resident scholar at the American Enterprise Institute for Public Policy Research, writes that successful candidates are those who can use the media to their full advantage.

As you read, consider the following questions:

1. According to the author, how have the media changed political campaigns in the 1980s?
2. Due to the dominance of television in modern elections, who has become the most important member of a campaign staff, in Ranney's opinion?
3. Why does Ranney believe that Nixon came across poorly on television?

The most obvious, though not necessarily the most important, respect in which television has changed the politician's world is its impact on electoral politics, both in the ways in which campaigns are conducted and in the kinds of candidates who do best under the camera's eye.

Politicians have long believed that face-to-face contact between politicians and voters is by far the most effective way to campaign. Many no doubt still believe it, but they all recognize that in the 1980s' world of mass constituencies and of voters who would rather stay home and watch television than attend a political rally in some auditorium, appearing on television is the closest candidates can get to all but a handful of their constituents and provides by far the most cost-effective campaigning device they have. Moreover, appearing on television is almost as good as appearing in person: politicians generally believe, with Kurt and Gladys Lang, that watching something on television makes people think "they 'see for themselves,' that they are directly involved in history, that television takes them to the scene, that they have a clearer picture of what is going on than people right 'there.'" Put another way, while eye-to-eye contact and a warm handshake between politician and voter may be best, having the politician's voice and face appear in living color on the tube a few feet away from the constituent in his own living room is surely second best.

Campaign Television

There are, of course, two forms of campaign television: "paid television," in which the campaign organization produces the equivalent of a commercial advertisement and pays the stations and networks to air them; and "free television," in which the broadcasters find what the candidate is doing and saying sufficiently interesting and newsworthy for them to broadcast it as part of their public affairs coverage in newscasts and interview slots in magazine shows. Both forms are vital to any well-run campaign in a large (national or statewide) constituency, but free television is generally thought to be the more desirable of the two, and not for budgetary reasons alone. As Larry Sabato puts it:

> Paid media gives certainty of control and flexibility, but it cannot match the unpaid media for credibility or, in most cases, for size and attentiveness of audience. The three networks' evening news now reaches an average of 28 million homes. The average local station, copying the national networks, is devoting more time to public affairs programs and hiring a far larger news staff. All political consultants fully acknowledge that the unpaid media, more than paid media, can make or break a candidate.

One result, according to Robert Agranoff, is that "the campaign must be planned and organized around the media schedule. The event to be covered must meet the news deadline of the radio and

TV stations." Another is that every campaign organization must have at least one (many have more) "media director" who is skilled at mounting and scheduling campaign events that will get maximum exposure on free television. This is a technical skill requiring both talent and experience, and people who have these skills usually sell them to campaign organizations for large fees. The same can be said for the professionals who manage the many other technical operations of modern campaigns, such as taking and analyzing public opinion polls, compiling computerized mailing lists of potential supporters and donors and sending them direct mail appeals, producing and purchasing time for televised political advertisements, and the like.

Scoring on the Evening News

In the campaign of 1984, there was no doubt that the single most important objective for a candidate was scoring well on the evening news shows on a particular night. Campaign managers closed their office doors at 6:30 or 7:00 every night to watch what "really" had happened that day. And if an event didn't happen on television, it didn't happen at all.

Jack W. Germond and Jules Witcover, *Wake Us When It's Over*, 1985.

There are, indeed, so many and varied technical skills needed to run a modern large-scale, television-centered campaign that the greatest need of all is for someone at the top to develop the strategy and tactics, to use them to the best advantage, and to coordinate all the technical specialists behind the master plan. Hardly any candidates or leaders of the parties' state or county organizations have the necessary know-how to do the top job, and so there has arisen a whole new profession of political consultants who have taken over the direction of most major campaigns. Some will work only for Democratic or Republican or liberal or conservative candidates, but more are "hired guns" who will work for any candidate who will pay their fees. Almost all of them, however, have in common the fact that their prepolitical experience has been in the fields of advertising and public relations, both heavily dependent on using the mass media, and not in the organizations and activities of political parties. A comprehensive list of the most successful political consultants would be far too long to publish here, but any such list would certainly include the names of Douglas Bailey, John Deardourff, David Garth, Joseph Napolitan, Matt Reese, and Stuart Spencer.

The point to note is that political consultants have also entirely replaced party politicians as the top organizers and strategists of large-scale political campaigns. That is a logical and probably inevitable consequence of the growing dominance of television in campaigning that, according to Anthony Smith, has taken place not only in the United States but in all Western-style democracies:

> Even before the microphone, the politician aimed his words through the crowd, not at it: his real target was the reporters' bench and the rows of shorthand books. The microphone made the politician aware of the vastness of the political space in which he operated and of the invisible audience to which he had to project himself. For a century the stuff of politics was tailored to the needs of the newspaper, and until a generation ago the newspaper was shaped by the requirements of politics. Out of the connection came a symbolic system of communication: the newspapers described debates, conflicts, demonstrations, activities. The innovation of television was actually to show personalities and events: to a large degree, the television coverage *is* the electoral campaign. . . .

Good on TV

If changing the rules changes the game, then every change of rules is likely to help some kinds of players and handicap others. Certainly the central role television has come to play in the game of mass-election politics has helped candidates who can afford to hire the very best in political consultants, media specialists, makeup artists, and prime-time exposure. But has it also given special advantages to candidates with other assets than money?

There is, as yet, no definitive answer to that question. However, many observers of television-age American politics have given their impressions, and they almost all agree that being "good on television" has become one of the first requirements (some say *the* first) for being a successful candidate for nomination and election to the presidency, a governorship, a seat in the U.S. Senate, or any office with a constituency that encompasses one or more television markets.

So much seems sensible, perhaps obvious. But what makes one aspirant good on television and another not so good? Some social science mass communications theory suggests some clues.

A "Cool" Medium?

Still the best known (though not best understood) of the modern mass communications theorists is the late Marshall McLuhan. One of his most familiar ideas is that television is a "cool" medium that, in politics, advantages "cool" candidates and handicaps "hot" ones. McLuhan defined the two categories thus:

> There is a basic principle that distinguishes . . . a hot medium like the movie from a cool one like TV. A hot medium is one that extends one single sense in "high definition." High definition is the state of being well filled with data. A photograph is, visually, "high definition." A cartoon is "low definition," simply because very little visual information is provided. . . . Hot

media are, therefore, low in participation, and cool media are high in participation or completion by the audience.

McLuhan argued from this premise that television is a cool medium because its pictures are of low definition compared with movies and photographs, its sound is of much lower fidelity than most radio and records, and all in all it leaves a good deal for the viewer to fill in. In politics, he continued, television is very hard on candidates with "hot" personalities, such as Senator Joseph McCarthy or Richard Nixon (McLuhan's illustrations). They both presented very strong and sharply defined partisan images, leaving few blank spaces for the viewers to fill with their own issue and personality preferences. . . .

We noted earlier that one of the prime objectives of every cam-

Danziger in The Christian Science Monitor © 1986 TCSPS.

paign for a public office with a large constituency is to get as much free and favorable exposure as possible on local and national newscasts and interview shows that are likely to be seen by the constituency's voters. Television news producers know very well that all manner of candidates are constantly trying to get such exposure, and they are wary of the possibility that their shows might serve a candidate's purposes more than the broadcasters'. Hence if they are convinced that a particular campaign event is a pure "mediality," manufactured out of whole cloth by some media consultant for free air time, they are likely to ignore it—unless, of course, it is just too audience-grabbing to pass up.

Gimmicks

Accordingly, one of the most valued tricks of the consultant's trade is knowing how to invent and stage campaign events that will serve *both* the broadcasters' needs for good visuals and newsworthiness *and* the candidate's need for free and favorable exposure. To that end the best consultants have come up with a variety of imaginative gimmicks. One of the most familiar is described by Larry Sabato:

> The "walking" candidate is a favorite. More than a quarter century ago an obscure Nevada journalist, Thomas Mechling, trekked across his state to upset the favored candidate for a Democratic U.S. Senate nomination. Trudging across a constituency became a successful tactic again in the early 1970s. First "walkin' Lawton" Chiles plodded his way 1,003 miles down the Florida penninsula to win a Senate seat in 1970. Then Dan Walker (appropriately named) became governor of Illinois, and Dick Clark upset an incumbent U.S. senator in Iowa in 1972 using the technique. After that the dam broke, and literally hundreds of candidates have, with varying degrees of success, joined the fad and put on their walking boots.

Another imaginative and successful gimmick was the "work day" approach invented by media consultant Robert Squier for an obscure Florida state senator, Bob Graham, in his campaign for the 1978 Democratic gubernatorial nomination. Squier arranged for Graham to work one day each at 100 mainly blue-collar jobs. During his lunch hour on the tenth day Graham called a press conference, announced his candidacy, and said his work days were intended to help him learn the real problems, thoughts, and feelings of the people of Florida. For each of the remaining ninety days he was followed by a number of reporters and often appeared on television newscasts. Squier also had his own cameras at the scenes, and in the paid advertisements he produced later he used film clips of Graham teaching a class while Graham's voice-over discussed his educational policies, clips of Graham driving a truck while Graham was giving his views on transportation policy, and

165

so on. It worked splendidly: Graham began as an unknown, but he finished second in the first round of the primary with 25 percent of the votes in a field of seven. He then won the runoff primary with 53 percent and the general election with 55 percent.

The Horse Race

This has its social costs, of course, not the least of which is a certain trivialization of the campaigns. Thomas Patterson's study of media coverage of the 1976 presidential election campaign found that nearly three-fifths of the networks' coverage dealt with the "horse race" aspects (who was gaining or losing, how campaign strategies were changing, the size of crowds at airport rallies and motorcades) and less than a third on substance (the candidates' stands on the issues and their records in prior offices). This was a higher proportion of trivia than in any of the newspapers and news magazines, but not much higher. . . .

High Cost of the Media

The emphasis on TV makes campaigns more expensive, because TV ads cost a lot of money. Therefore candidates have to devote enormous amounts of time to raising money, especially money from political action committees. They are so busy hustling for dollars that their time for meeting and talking with ordinary citizens is limited. Candidates from both parties often find themselves competing for the favor of the same corporate givers. This tends to blur their differences on the big issues. The danger is not only that candidates will become ideologically conservative but also that they will grow politically cautious, shying away from risks that might offend their contributors.

The New Republic, November 3, 1986.

Politicians, in public office or out, have no doubt that, like it or not, they have to operate in a world in which political reality for most people is what television says it is. They are well aware of television's great power not only to make life difficult for them but also to enable them to bring their messages and personalities to far more people far more effectively than they can by any other means. So they do their best, often with success, to use both paid and free television exposure for their own ends.

In short, television and politicians are in a symbiotic as well as an adversarial relationship because they need each other. Their relationship is always uneasy and often quarrelsome, but it is permanent. And it sets many of the most important circumstances within which governing in America must be conducted.

"TV and the media in general increasingly may dictate the nature of campaigns. But the politicians remain the power brokers."

The Media Have Little Impact on US Elections

Lewis W. Wolfson

The media have made celebrities out of politicians and politicians out of celebrities. Actor Ronald Reagan became president. Movie star Clint Eastwood became a mayor. And political figure G. Gordon Liddy appeared on *Miami Vice*. Despite this overlapping of media popularity and political power, Lewis W. Wolfson believes the media do not create political leaders, they merely reflect a politician's climb to power. In the following viewpoint, Wolfson, professor of communication at The American University in Washington, writes that media influence in elections is greatly exaggerated and that politicians control the media, not vice versa.

As you read, consider the following questions:

1. In the author's opinion, how did the 1980 presidential campaign prove that media influence is greatly exaggerated?
2. According to Wolfson, do the media give an accurate picture of who the candidates really are?
3. Does Wolfson think political advertising is effective? Why or why not?

Reporting on elections and politics may be journalists' greatest labor of love. It is also a continuing source of anguish. Every two or four years newspeople joyously thrust themselves into covering political campaigns. They provide more information about them than the press anywhere else in the world. But when the shouting is over, the media keep having to explain why they told us too much about some things, not enough about others, and sometimes were simply wrong.

Critics say the news media tell us too much about the horse race, campaign tactics, and narrow issues, and not enough about the candidates' capabilities to govern. Elections, which are supposed to be a dialogue with the voters, often sound more like the politicians and journalists talking to each other. We may lose sight of the point of it all. Government itself sometimes seems like something "separate and incidental" to the "election game."

The news media unquestionably shape elections, but there is hot debate over just what their influence is. Journalist Theodore White says they have "sweeping political power." Political scientists call them the new power brokers, rivaling the parties themselves in their ability to decide who the candidates will be, how the public perceives them, and who ultimately wins. "The old worry was that the politicians [would] dominate reporters, brandishing the sword of state; the new worry is that reporters dominate politicians, ruling the rulers with their pens," writes one critic.

The Real Power Brokers

Anyone who deals with the realities of politics knows better. TV and the media in general increasingly may dictate the nature of campaigns. But the politicians remain the power brokers. They set the agenda of issues, create campaign events, and try to use the media to fashion a winning image. Skillful ones like Ronald Reagan can even co-opt TV news for that purpose. But the media themselves don't lust after power. Publishers and broadcast owners don't yearn to be kingmakers the way press barons like William Randolph Hearst and Joseph Pulitzer did. Reporters know that a hint of partisanship will undermine their credibility.

The media don't tell us how to think and vote. But we do want to know what's at stake in an election, and what our choices are. To their credit, the media do considerable planning in this area of coverage. Yet newspeople still get caught up in the spectacle and surprises. They reach after fleeting stories despite themselves. They venture unwise predictions and may be stunned by the outcome. They forswear yesterday's errors, yet many commit new ones. "Let us be modest, ladies and gentlemen," David Broder tells his colleagues, "for we have much to be modest about."

Analyst Jeff Greenfield says the 1980 presidential campaign

showed dramatically how the news media's power in elections can be "vastly exaggerated." There were "sudden bursts of momentum that led nowhere, press coverage of candidates that twisted and turned so frequently as to be self-nullifying, elaborate and expensive advertising campaigns that had nothing to do with the success of the candidates," he said. Press attention preserves the openness of elections and can force healthy political debate. News organizations do serious analysis. But the lack of selectivity in coverage is a problem. We are flooded with information, but crave perspective. Instead of educating voters, the news media may cause some of them to tune out.

Citizens *Use* the Media

Although it is reasonable to suspect that impressions are shaped by the news (where else could they come from?) and there is some evidence that news coverage shapes impressions of candidates, attempts to untangle the effect of particular news sources have generally failed. . . . Furthermore, there is evidence that citizens *use* (rather than *are affected by*) news reports to expand, refine, and fill in existing belief systems in a process that is complex and varied.

Richard Joslyn, *Mass Media and Elections*, 1984.

Does the press decide elections? There are as many possible reasons for the outcome of an election as fishes in a pond, and journalists' "frantic energies" may have little to do with it, as Greenfield says. The news media are simply one element in an often surprising and uncontrollable political decision making process. As one veteran journalist has put it, the American people "have a remarkable genius for reading, listening, watching and then making up their own minds in some strange and independent way."

Reporting on Elections

For all its faults, political reporting has improved immensely in recent years. Many news organizations have invested considerable resources in coverage. They have been fairer in allocating space and time to candidates. Newspapers let their editorial biases influence the news columns far less than they once did. Broadcasters have provided free time for the candidates to talk to voters and debate their opponents. Reporters have explored party reforms, campaign management, and the influence of money in politics. If the amount of coverage were all that counted, you would have to say that the press serves democracy admirably.

Yet, newspeople tend to treat elections as narrow tests of imagery and footwork: Can the candidate get the voters' attention and make it through the campaign without shooting himself or herself in the foot? We find out less about "who the candidates really are and what they are trying to do and say," as Jim Perry of the *Wall Street Journal* puts it. "Often, it seems, that is what interests us least; it is what should motivate us most." The issues political journalists concentrate on most may melt away after the election is over. The news media cannot regularly look back and say, "We did it! We told voters what the candidates are really like and what the choices are. We plumbed the key issues, the concerns that were on people's minds and that the winners will have to face up to. We got the voters more involved."

To prepare for elections, larger news outlets have at least one reporter whose job is to keep watch on politics year round—the parties, the potential candidates, campaign spending. Below the national level, politics usually is reported by state capitol, city hall, or general assignment reporters who are joined by colleagues as the election nears. In smaller communities, a single reporter will have to cover all elections—for mayor, city or town council, school board, and the state legislature, as well as referenda.

Never-Ending Campaigns

The process is never-ending. A presidential campaign begins with scarcely a respite after the last one. For other offices, party primaries can crowd the calendar from early in the election year on; and in states where one party dominates, the primaries *are* the election. It is a grueling process for the reporter. He or she will be proud about spending so much money and manpower to keep track of a Reagan election landslide that was rarely, if ever, in doubt.

The press ought to be policing the horse race game; instead it is a co-conspirator. Political scientist Larry Sabato says the hoopla about polls should be deflated "to a point more in keeping with their real significance and usefulness," and we ought to be constantly reminded of their shortcomings. The pollsters won't do this because they have too much of a stake in their trade; so, says Sabato, it is up to the politicians and the press to talk more about bold leadership rather than constantly trying to find out which way the wind is blowing.

Television's Role

Nothing is more talked about, debated, celebrated, and condemned in politics these days than the role of TV. Is TV the answer to a politician's prayers? Does it decide elections? No one is quite ready to say it does, though no one doubts its overall impact on the political process. David Broder says, "Television has probably changed American politics more than any other single factor" in recent times. Longtime political adviser Frederick Dutton says the effects of TV on politics have been "overwhelming." It has altered the parties and the whole nominating process. It has lessened voters' party loyalties and changed their approach to elections by playing so heavily on their "impressions, appetites and impulses."

TV has created a generation of politicians who worry as much about wearing the right colored shirt for the cameras as about what they have to say on the issues. A cadre of political consultants keep them worrying. TV also has created a new cottage industry for political scientists, who for years virtually ignored the media's impact on the political process. Now they have become entranced with their power.

Political Advertising

Though TV is not so new any more, it remains a novelty to many who watch campaigns. Political advertising's impact is hotly debated. In 1968, a young man named Joe McGinniss worked his way into Richard Nixon's presidential campaign. He later wrote a sensational exposé of how television advertising was used to try to sell Nixon to us as president. McGinniss pictured campaign aids as shaping a new image for the man who had been dogged by his TV "loss" to John Kennedy in the 1960 debates. "It's not what's there that counts; it's what's projected," wrote Nixon adviser Ray Price in a campaign memo. The old Nixon—"tricky Dick" with the cartoonists' five o'clock shadow and the political hatchet— was to be replaced by an image of Nixon as "the kind of man proud parents would ideally want their sons to grow up to be [like]: a man who embodies the national ideal, its aspirations, its dreams."

The Myth of TV Influence

Part of the folklore born in [the 1984] election is that Mr. Reagan won only because of television. His smile, charm and generalities were supposed to play well. Indeed, they did play well, but it is patronizing to the people who voted for Mr. Reagan to say they did so only because they were beguiled. It supposes that Americans perceive government and politics the same way they do *Dallas*.

Perhaps they do, of course, but how do we explain Richard M. Nixon? He was the least telegenic candidate imaginable, and he seemed to dislike television as much as Mr. Mondale. Nonetheless, he beat George McGovern, a personable man, with 61% of the vote. Mr. Reagan, the Great Communicator, only got 59%.

Don Fry, *Believing the News*, 1985.

Was Nixon sold to us? Can candidates be marketed like light beer and deodorant? Some consultants say proudly that is exactly what they try to do, while others talk about a loftier process of "political communication." It is not certain what the ad campaign did for Nixon in 1968, especially since he came close to losing. But the McGinniss book caught journalists by surprise; they had not paid much attention to the "other" campaign on TV. There followed an avalanche of press speculation about the advent of a new era in politics. The imagemakers—the media consultants—would be the new kingmakers. They could make a silk purse out of a sow's ear or a horse's tail. The parties would be bypassed and a new kind of candidate would go directly to the people on TV. "It is possible, though hardly to be cheered, that candidates may never even have to leave sterile, air-conditioned studios and face the spontaneity and danger of live audiences that have not been computer selected," Frederick Dutton wrote.

Spending Millions To Go Nowhere

It didn't happen. Millions of dollars have been spent on TV, mostly on presidential, congressional, and gubernatorial races; some candidates have been "made" by television, but others have gone nowhere. TV advertising can give a candidate quick recognition of his or her name and face. It sometimes can reinforce the image a politician seeks to create of himself or herself. It can counter an opponent's ads. It can be an effective device for attacking, though the attacks can backfire.

But sometimes paid TV exposure gives a campaign only a small boost or none at all. "When you've been in enough different campaigns, you find out that in some cases television is not very important at all," says Charles Guggenheim, a leading political filmmaker. Are we media wizards? asks sought-after consultant Robert Squier wryly: "Go talk to some of the candidates who have lost that we have worked for." TV political ads can be informative, as some studies show; but some think the barrage of them may do as much to deaden voter interest as to stimulate it.

"Broadcast television imposes limits . . . on explicit sex. Why not on explicit terror?"

The Media Aid Terrorists

Charles Krauthammer

When does a spectator become an accessory to a crime? Many critics of the media believe that extensive coverage of terrorism aids terrorists by providing free publicity for their actions. Charles Krauthammer, a nationally-syndicated columnist, thinks the media have covered terrorism irresponsibly. In the following viewpoint, Krauthammer writes that the media must impose self-enforced limits on their coverage of terrorism to help end the carnage.

As you read, consider the following questions:

1. According to the author, why is journalism ill-suited to cover evil acts, specifically terrorism?
2. How do the media "create" reality, in Krauthammer's opinion?
3. What does he suggest the media do to improve their coverage of terrorism?

The problem of evil has long been the province of philosophy. Philosophy is not particularly interested in that question anymore. (Nor is the world much interested in philosophy, but that is another matter.) Journalism has taken up the slack. Unfortunately, journalism is not terribly well equipped to handle it, principally because journalism is a medium of display and demonstration. When evil is the subject, the urge to display leads to dark places indeed. . . .

[In June of 1985], for example, it led to Osaka, Japan, where reporters and photographers stood around while two men broke into the apartment of an accused swindler, murdered him with 13 bayonet stabs, then emerged blood splattered to a press corps stunned, but not too stunned to keep the TV cameras rolling. It led to West Germany, where a couple of magazines, *Bunte Illustrierte* and *Stern*, tried to auction off to other media bits of Mengele, photographs, letters and other memorabilia. Finally, it led to Beirut, where during 17 days of astonishing symbiosis, television and terrorists co-produced—there is no better word—a hostage drama.

For journalism, as for the other performing arts, evil is a fascinating and indispensable subject. The question is how to fix on the subject without merging with it. For many arts, the solution is to interpose time: their reflections on evil are, for the most part, recollections in tranquillity. On television news, that protective distance disappears.

No event has demonstrated the bizarre consequences of that fact quite as dramatically as the TWA hijacking. There, under laboratory conditions, journalism met terror, in a pure culture, uncontaminated by civilization. The results are not encouraging. Terror needed a partner in crime to give the event life. The media, television above all, obliged.

Driven not by malevolence but by those two journalistic imperatives, technology and competition, journalism will go where it can go. When it has the technology, it shoots first and asks questions later. For the correspondent bargaining for access to hostages, the important questions are Can I get the story/show? and Will anyone else? The question What am I doing? comes up after the tape has been relayed from Damascus, if at all.

As a result, others ask the question and produce a depressingly familiar list of findings: insensitivity to the families; exploitation of the hostages; absurd, degrading deference to jailers; interference with diplomacy; appropriation of the role of negotiator. (David Hartman to Nabih Berri: "Any final words to President Reagan this morning?") And finally, giving over the airwaves to people whose claim to airtime is based entirely on the fact that they are forcibly holding innocent Americans.

The principal defense against these charges is perhaps best

called the cult of objectivity. Journalists are led to believe, and some may actually believe, that they only hold a mirror to life. And mirrors can hardly be accused of bad faith. After all, the idea of neutrality inheres in the very word medium. There is a story out there to be got, and as Sam Donaldson, prominent preacher of this doctrine, puts it, "It's our job to cover the story . . . we bring information."

Not even physicists, practitioners of a somewhat more exact science, have so arrogant a belief in the out there. For 60 years, physics has learned to live with its Uncertainty Principle: that the act of observing an event alters its nature. Journalism continues to resist the idea.

And journalism, which shines lights at people, not electrons, does more than alter. It creates. First, out of the infinite flotsam of "events" out there, it makes "stories." Then, by exposing them (and their attached people, ideas, crimes), it puts them on the map. "As seen on TV" gives substance to murder as surely as it does to Ginzu knives. The parade of artifacts is varied, but the effect is the same: coverage makes them real.

No one knows this better than terrorists. No one is more grudging in acknowledging this than television journalists. Their self-criticism takes place generally at the periphery. For example, the

John Trever, reprinted with permission.

TV anchors were much embarrassed that reporters' unruliness caused the first hostage press conference to be temporarily called off. (By terrorists, mind you.) But that misses the point. The real point is what they were doing when not unruly: blanketing American airwaves with shows choreographed by the captors, with the hostages, under constant but concealed threat, acting as their spokesmen.

Another fine point was whether to run live pictures. Dan Rather said no, averring that his network would not be handed over to terrorists. This was in contrast to ABC, which had broadcast live interviews. But what purpose does it serve to broadcast these interviews at all? If the purpose is to show that the hostages are alive and well, the tools of the print media—a still picture and a summary of what had happened—are perfectly adequate. But that would be bad television. And that is exactly the point: the play's the thing. These terrorist productions are coveted for their dramatic, not their news value.

That realization might open the way to some solution, or at least some approach to the problem of reducing terrorist control of the airwaves. If much of the coverage is indeed not news but entertainment—bizarre guerrilla theater that outdoes *Network*—then television might quite properly place voluntary limits on it, as it does on other entertainments.

Broadcast television imposes limits, strict but self-enforced limits, on explicit sex. Why not on explicit terror? There is no reason why all the news of a terrorist event, like news of a rape, cannot be transmitted in some form. But in the interest of decency, diplomacy and our own self-respect, it need not be live melodrama.

A few years ago, when some publicity seekers started dashing onto baseball fields during televised games, TV producers decided to discourage the practice by averting the camera's eye. So now, the crowd roars at the commotion, and the viewer strains to see what it is all about, but cannot. Yet he accepts this restraint, this self-censorship, if you will, without complaint because it serves to avoid delays at ball games. Yet we won't do the same when the end is reducing the payoff for political murder.

If we did the same, the drama we would miss would no doubt be riveting. Evil is riveting. From watching Hitchcock we know of the perverse, and fully human, enjoyment that comes from looking evil dead in the eye. But when the evil is real and the suffering actual, that enjoyment is tinged with shame, the kind of shame one experiences when exposed to pornography.

And like pornography, terrorist television, the graphic unfolding of evil on camera, sells. During the hostage crisis, network news ratings rose markedly. But this fascination has its price. Lot's wife fixed her gaze on evil and turned to salt.

"The . . . pain of captives and family has come not from TV cameras and anchorpeople . . . but from the faltering will of governments."

The Media Do Not Aid Terrorists

A.M. Rosenthal and Jonathan Harris

Anyone who has seen images of shattered bodies and grief-stricken families will not soon forget the terrible toll of terrorism. However, did the media simply report those events, or were they partially responsible for them? Those who support freedom of the press state that journalists only mirror reality, they do not create it. In Part I of the following two-part viewpoint, A.M. Rosenthal, editor of *The New York Times*, writes that terrorism is caused more by weak-willed governments than by the media. In Part II, Jonathan Harris, an expert on international relations, states that terrorism is a legitimate news event that must be covered.

As you read, consider the following questions:

1. According to Rosenthal, how have governments become weak-willed in handling terrorism?
2. Rosenthal writes that most TV journalists are professional. How then does he explain TV's poor image?
3. What evidence does Harris give to prove that the networks are careful about covering terrorism?

I

Next week a plane will be hijacked and the passengers, many of them American, will be taken hostage.

If not next week, it will happen the week after or next month or the month after that. But it will happen.

Terrorism, old in warfare, has been developed by nationalist and carefully nurtured religious fanaticism to the point where it is a weapon, not simply of local resistance but of world importance. The terrorists have discovered that it is far more effective to select victims from the nationals of foreign powers rather than concentrate merely on their specific enemies.

Nothing gets them more attention and blackmail power than the horror of a hijacking, not even the kidnappings taking place now in Beirut.

And most of the victim nations have shown they will crack when hostages are taken. The United States cracked to Soviet hostage taking by trading a Soviet spy for an American newsman and then delivered blackmail arms to Iran, sponsors of the killers of U.S. Marines. Pakistan has yet to put hijackers captured [in 1986] . . . on trial or even tell who they are.

Other Cracks

Israel cracked by turning over 1,150 prisoners for three Israelis. The Italians let a hunted terrorist escape, the French dealt almost openly in trading with terrorists for their hostages.

Anybody who says this contemptuously is a fool. We all know that were one of our family taken hostage we would want only one thing of our government—rescue. But the surrenders do lead, bitterly, to more hostage taking and more pain for more families.

Once again the frightened faces of the victims will appear on TV screens the world over. And once again the captors will orchestrate their own performance on the TV stage, screaming and waving automatic rifles one day, presenting their demands and their grievances as winningly as they can the next.

Once more disgusted viewers and harassed governments will say that the press, particularly TV, is terrorism's tool and endangering the lives of the hostages. Louder than ever will come demands for some form of regulation—outright censorship, barring reporters and cameras from the scene, or sweeping press self-restriction.

TV and newspaper people talked it over at a meeting . . . organized by the Poynter Institute for Media Studies, which owns the St. Petersburg Times, one of the country's good newspapers.

Media Coverage

The question on our minds was whether the long, wearing hijacking coverage in Beirut in 1985 had endangered the lives of the hostages or made freeing the captives more difficult. To his

BERRY'S WORLD By Jim Berry

WHEN IN DOUBT, BLAME THE MEDIA

© 1986 by NEA, Inc.

Jim Berry. Reprinted by permission of Newspaper Enterprise Association.

professional credit, Parker Borg, a State Department anti-terrorism expert at the time, said the answer was no.

But during next week's or next month's hostage taking, the debate will start all over again. TV does not enjoy all the First Amendment protections—I believe it should—and the pressure will be heavy.

There are things that can be done that would not damage the right of TV to present the news fully and would help prevent it from becoming the most important hostage of all.

Occasionally the gunmen get control of TV by being broadcast live, from the scene of the crime right into the living room, spouting whatever they wish to spout. This is exactly as if gunmen marched into a newspaper office and dictated to reporters and editors every word that was to appear in print. Pausing to see and edit tapes in advance is no more an act of censorship than a newspaper editor taking a look at a story before it is printed and using something called judgment.

Terrorists feed hungrily on chaos and press-TV mob scenes create the hysteria they seek. TV could help by using correspondents but just one or two camera crews, sharing film but not the reporting or commentary.

Almost all TV anchormen and producers are skilled, experienced and serious and could hold down top jobs on newspapers; greater praise hath no editor. But sometimes the job of interviewing captors is turned over to TV personalities who are simply entertainers and treat the captors as statesmen: "Do you have a message for President Reagan?"

These steps will counter some of the intricately planned manipulation by the terrorists. But TV and press bashing will continue; it won't kill us.

Neither will it change the fact that the agonizingly drawn-out pain of captives and family has come not from TV cameras and anchorpeople or newspaper reporters but from the faltering will of governments and the men you see waving their rifles and sneering at the world, next week or next month.

II

The role of the media in terrorist crises has become a subject of heated dispute, with calls for strict government controls countered by pleas invoking the freedom of the press.

In the words of a 1979 report by a committee of the U.S. House of Representatives, the media have sometimes been guilty of "grossly sensationalized reporting." When this occurs, it can "inflame the incident and exaggerate the terrorists' power and influence.". . .

Legitimate News Events

Yet there are serious questions as to the possible effects of downplaying or ignoring terrorist incidents. Unchecked rumors could spread panic among the general public. Terrorists might escalate their violence to a level that could not be ignored in order to compel the public attention they seek.

Terrorist attacks are legitimate news events. The public does have a right to know. The problem lies in establishing proper safeguards so that news stories about such incidents are presented in a rational manner that neither encourages nor exaggerates terrorism.

The media are well aware of the problem and have attempted to respond to it in ways that would make government censorship unnecessary. A 1978 statement by NBC News to a subcommittee of the House Committee on the Judiciary presented a balanced view:

> NBC News has adopted flexible guidelines. . . . We must act with care not to exacerbate any terrorist situation . . . nor to be "used" or manipulated by any of the principals. Our job is to report the essential information without sensationalizing the event.

NBC pledged never to broadcast any terrorist incident live

without special permission. Its news people were never to "participate in any way, especially by interviewing kidnappers or hostages during the incident," without first consulting the authorities.

> Because ours is a democratic society, we live by the premise that the benefits of freedom of speech should outweigh the risks of disclosure. Indeed, coverage of a terrorist incident might plant an idea in someone's head to imitate those acts. . . . However, a news organization must balance the public's right to know against that risk.

CBS News stated to the subcommittee that, "In such volatile situations, responsibility must be exercised by news organizations so that the danger to human life inherent in terrorist incidents" is not heightened. CBS contended that

> governmental efforts to suppress newsworthy information raise the most serious constitutional questions. . . . We believe that the public is best served by full and factual reporting of terrorist incidents.

At the same time, CBS reported that it had adopted guidelines regulating its coverage. Virtually all American news organizations have done so within the past few years.

Understanding Words in Context

Readers occasionally come across words which they do not recognize. And frequently, because they do not know a word or words, they will not fully understand the passage being read. Obviously, the reader can look up an unfamiliar word in a dictionary. By carefully examining the word in the context in which it is used, however, the word's meaning can often be determined. A careful reader may find clues to the meaning of the word in surrounding words, ideas, and attitudes.

Below are excerpts from the viewpoints in this chapter. In each excerpt one or two words are printed in italics. Try to determine the meaning of each word by reading the excerpt. Under each excerpt you will find four definitions for the italicized word. Choose the one that is closest to your understanding of the word.

Finally, use a dictionary to see how well you have understood the words in context. It will be helpful to discuss with others the clues which helped you decide on each word's meaning.

1. We should be more resistant than ever to media hype—the *PSEUDOEVENT*, the staged protest, the packaged candidate, the prime-time announcement and the televised interview.

   PSEUDOEVENT means:

   a) psychic occurrence
   b) gala celebration
   c) fake news
   d) foreign politics

2. I saw a senator call a press conference for what I felt was a *PEDAGOGICAL* purpose, trying to educate reporters to the importance or intricacies of an issue.

   PEDAGOGICAL means:

   a) presumptuous
   b) educational
   c) childish
   d) pedestrian

3. In Beirut, during 17 days of astonishing *SYMBIOSIS*, television and terrorists co-produced a hostage drama.

   SYMBIOSIS means:

   a) mutual dependence   c) spurred growth
   b) theatre   d) tension

4. The principal defense against charges of favoritism is best called the cult of *OBJECTIVITY.*

   OBJECTIVITY means:

   a) blind prejudice   c) religion
   b) things   d) without personal
        bias

5. The media have been guilty of grossly *SENSATIONALIZED* political reporting. These hyped stories can needlessly inflame incidents and exaggerate the terrorists' power.

   SENSATIONALIZED means:

   a) great   c) overblown
   b) touching   d) violent

6. We not only look on the government with the healthy skepticism of journalists. We also have a hard, intensely *ADVERSARIAL* attitude.

   ADVERSARIAL means:

   a) negative   c) strong opponent
   b) belligerent   d) proponent

7. Political scientists call the media the new *POWER BROKERS*, rivaling the political parties themselves in their ability to decide who wins elections.

   POWER BROKERS means:

   a) stockmarket players   c) thugs
   b) people with influence   d) energy plants

8. Appearing on television is the closest candidates can get to their *CONSTITUENTS* and provides the most cost-effective campaigning device they have.

   CONSTITUENTS means:

   a) payroll   c) represented citizens
   b) colleagues   d) congressional
        district

Periodical Bibliography

The following articles have been selected to supplement the diverse views expressed in this chapter.

Russell Baker	"Read Us Some More of That TV," *The New York Times*, December 31, 1986.
William J. Casey	"Conquering the Cancer of Terrorism," *USA Today*, November 1986.
The Center Magazine	March/April 1987, entire issue. Available from PO Box 4068, Santa Barbara, CA 93140.
Rushworth M. Kidder	"Unmasking Terrorism: Manipulation of the Media," *The Christian Science Monitor*, May 16, 1986.
Robert Karl Manoff	"The 'Nightline' Line," *The Progressive*, December 1986.
Colman McCarthy	"Wrong from the Start," *The Washington Post National Weekly Edition*, December 15, 1986.
Ruth J. Moss	"Candidate Camera," *Psychology Today*, December 1986.
Ralph Nader	"Why Voter Turnout Is Turning Off: Candidates Avoid the Public," *The New York Times*, November 4, 1986.
The New Republic	"The $676,000 Clean-Up," December 1, 1986.
Michael J. O'Neill	"TV Dominating Government," *USA Today*, April 1986.
Thomas Patterson	"Television and the Decline of Politics," *Kettering Review*, Winter 1987.
Christopher Swan	"Kalb To Lead Exploration into Media's Impact on Public Policy," *The Christian Science Monitor*, April 30, 1987.
U.S. News & World Report	"Boos Pelt the Press Box," May 19, 1986.
James M. Wall	"Culture Clashes Need Cautious Interpretation," *The Christian Century*, April 16, 1986.
William Zimmerman	"On Negative Ads," *The New York Times*, November 13, 1986.

Is Advertising Harmful to Society?

the **MASS MEDIA**

Chapter Preface

Whether one watches television, listens to the radio, reads magazines, or attends movies, one is exposed to advertising. Some critics of advertising's influence believe the government should regulate its content. Civil libertarians, on the other hand, argue that government interference would be censorship, violating the First Amendment rights of advertisers.

US government regulators have determined that advertising, unlike other forms of communication, does not merit full First Amendment protection. The 1970 congressional decision to ban all cigarette advertising from television confirmed this belief.

Anti-censorship groups, such as the American Civil Liberties Union, oppose *any* regulations which restrict advertising. They believe that Americans are intelligent enough to make their own decisions when exposed to advertising. They argue that government regulations are a form of censorship, which a democratic society cannot allow in any form.

The authors in this chapter discuss what role the government should play in advertising's future.

"The world of mass advertising teaches us that want and frustration are caused by our own deficiencies."

Advertising Has a Negative Effect on Society

Michael Parenti

Advertisements bombard the public from radios, televisions, billboards, and newspapers. What effect does this information have on society? Critics say the public's perception of reality is warped by the wanton materialism, sexism, and stereotypes portrayed in mass advertising. In the following viewpoint, Michael Parenti, a liberal and the author of *Power and the Powerless*, writes that mass advertising creates a value system based on consumption. He believes that advertisers not only market their products, but sell a complete way of life.

As you read, consider the following questions:

1. According to the author, what is the true objective of the media?
2. Parenti believes that advertisements sell more than products. What else do they sell?
3. In Parenti's opinion, how does big business portray itself as the Grand Provider?

Much of our media experience is neither news nor entertainment. Some 60 to 80 percent of newspaper space and about 22 percent of television time (even more on radio) is devoted to advertising. The average viewer who watches four hours of television daily, sees at least 100 to 120 commercials a day, or 36,400 to 43,680 a year. Many of the images in our heads, the expressions in our conversation, the jingles and tunes we hum, and, of course, the products we find ourselves using, are from the world of the Big Sell. Advertising not only urges products upon us, we in part become one of its products. We are, if anything, consumers. And even if we have learned to turn away from the television set when commercials come on and pass over the eye-catching ads in our newspapers and magazines, we cannot hope to remain untouched by the persistent, ubiquitous bombardment.

Most of us think of advertising as the sideshow we must tolerate in order to experience the media's more substantial offerings. Advertising picks up most of the costs of newspapers and magazines and all the costs of radio and television. Thus it is thought of as a means to an end. But a moment's reflection should tell us it is the other way round: The media's content, the news and entertainment, the features and "specials," are really the *means*, the lures to get us exposed to the advertisements. ("Journalists," said one press representative, "are just people who write on the back of advertisements.") The *end* is the advertising, the process of inducing people to spend as much money as possible on consumer products and services. Entertainment and news are merely instrumental to the goal of the advertiser. They are there to win audiences for the advertisers, to keep people tuned in and turned on. The objective is commercial gain, the sale of mass-produced goods to a mass market; only for that reason are advertisers willing to pay enormous sums for what passes as entertainment and news.

The Dawn of Mass Advertising

Mass advertising has not always been with us. It grew with mass media, or rather mass media grew with *it*. Mass advertising was a response to significant transformations in the productive system. The growth of modern technology and mass production brought changes in the lives of millions of Americans. The small community with its local economy and homebred recreational and cultural life gave way to an urbanized, industrial society of people who were obliged to turn more and more to a mass commodity market.

The age of mass consumption came to the United States most visibly in the 1920s, interrupted by the Great Depression and World War II, then exploding upon us with accumulated vigor in the postwar era. With it came the advertising industry, called into being by the economic imperative of having to market vast quantities of consumer goods and services. Among the new products were those that enabled advertising itself to happen: the penny-press newspaper, the low-priced slick magazine, the radio, and finally the television set—all in their turn were to become both mass consumption items and prime conduits for mass consumption advertising. Today the family and local community are no longer the primary units for production, recreation, self-definition, or even personal loyalty. Self-images, role models, and emotional attachments are increasingly sought from those whose specialty is to produce and manipulate images and from the images themselves.

BY MARLETTE FOR THE CHARLOTTE OBSERVER

"... AND NOW A WORD FROM OUR SPONSOR..."

Doug Marlette, reprinted with permission.

The obvious purpose of ads and commercials is to sell goods and services, but advertisers do more than that. Over and above any particular product, they sell an entire way of life, a way of experiencing social reality that is compatible with the needs of a mass-production, mass-consumption, capitalist society. Media advertising is both a propagator and a product of a consumer ideology.

Modern Consumerism

People have always had to consume in order to live, and in every class society, consumption styles have been a measure of one's status. But modern consumerism is a relatively recent development in which masses of people seek to accumulate things other than what they need and often other than what they can truly enjoy. Consumption is no longer just a means to life but a meaning for life. This is the essence of the consumer ideology. As propagated through mass advertising, the ideology standardizes tastes and legitimizes both the products of the system and the system itself, representing the commodity-ridden life as "the good life" and "the American Way." The consumer ideology, or consumerism, builds a mass psychology of "moreness" that knows no limit; hence the increase in material abundance ironically also can bring a heightened sense of scarcity and a sense of unfulfilled acquisition.

Advertisements often do not explicitly urge the consumer to buy a given product, rather they promise that the product will enhance a person's life, opening a whole range of desiderata including youthfulness, attractiveness, social grace, security, success, conviviality, sex, romance, and the admiration of others. Strictly speaking the advertisement does not *sell* the product as such. Rarely does the television commercial say "Buy Pepsi"; instead it urges us to "Join the Pepsi Generation."

Most consumers, if questioned on the matter, would agree that many commercials are exaggerated, unrealistic, and even untrue; but this skepticism does not immunize them from the advertisement hype. One can be critical of a particular commercial yet be swayed by it at some subliminal level, or by the overall impact of watching a thousand commercials a week. Thus millions of people bought high-priced designer jeans even if few actually believed the product would win them entry into that never-never world of slim-hipped glamorous people who joyfully wiggled their blue-denim posteriors into the TV camera, in an endless succession of commercials during the early 1980s.

The consumer ideology not only fabricates false needs, it panders in a false way to real ones. The desire for companionship, love, approval, and pleasure, the need to escape from drudgery and boredom, the search for security for oneself and one's family, such things are vital human concerns. The consumer ideology does something more pernicious than just activate our urge for conspicuous consumption; like so much else in the media and like other forms of false consciousness, consumerism plays on real human needs in deceptive and ultimately unfulfilling ways.

The Gospel of Advertising

One of the goals of advertising is to turn the consumer's critical perception away from the product—and away from the system that produces it—and toward herself or himself. Many commercials characterize people as loudmouthed imbeciles whose problems are solved when they encounter the right medication, cosmetic, cleanser, or gadget. In this way industry confines the social imagination and cultural experience of millions, teaching people to define their needs and life styles according to the dictates of the commodity market.

The reader of advertising copy and the viewer of commercials discover that they are not doing right for baby's needs or hubby's or wifey's desires; that they are failing in their careers because of poor appearance, sloppy dress, or bad breath; that they are not treating their complexion, hair, or nails properly; that they suffer unnecessary cold misery and headache pains; that they don't know how to make the tastiest coffee, pie, pudding, or chicken dinner; nor, if left to their own devices, would they be able to clean their floors, sinks, and toilets correctly or tend to their lawns, gardens, appliances, and automobiles. In order to live well and live properly, consumers need corporate producers to guide them. Consumers are taught personal incompetence and dependence on mass-market producers.

Why Bad Advertising Is Bad

- It teaches false values. By emphasizing a life based on "getting things" through instant gratification, there is an erosion of the true values of outgoing effort and concern, discipline and responsibility. . . .

- It encourages selfishness. This fostering of desire for "things" encourages people to *want* more—instead of trying to *be* more the way decent people should be.

- It corrupts personal relationships. The sexual exploitation of women in advertising is contributing to the growing failure of true man-woman relationships. To show that "love" is dependent upon some gadget (deodorant spray, soap or toothpaste) is misinformation and a simplification of life's complex interpersonal attitudes.

Graemme J. Marshall, *The Plain Truth*, November/December 1986.

Are people worried about the security of their homes and families? No need to fear, Prudential or All-State will watch over them. Are people experiencing loneliness? Ma Bell brings distant loved ones to them with a telephone call. The corporate system knows what formulas to feed your infants, what foods to feed your family, what medication to feed your cold, what gas to feed your engine, and how best to please your spouse, your boss, or your peers. Just as the mass market replaced family and community as provider of goods and services, so now corporations replace parents, grandparents, midwives, neighbors, craftspeople, and oneself in knowing what is best. Big business enhances its legitimacy and social hegemony by portraying itself as society's Grand Provider.

The world of mass advertising teaches us that want and frustration are caused by our own deficiencies. The goods are within easy reach, before our very eyes in dazzling abundance, available not only to the rich but to millions of ordinary citizens. Those unable to partake of this cornucopia have only themselves to blame. If you cannot afford to buy these things, goes the implicit message, the failure is yours and not the system's. The advertisement of consumer wares, then, is also an advertisement for a whole capitalist system, a demonstration that the system can deliver both the goods and the good life to everyone save laggards and incompetents.

"Advertising's actual effects are . . . not clearly known."

Advertising Has Little Effect on Society

Clifford G. Christians, Kim B. Rotzoll, and Mark Fackler

Advertising is pervasive. However, advertising's influence is not pervasive, according to some experts in communication. They contend that the sheer volume of mass advertising dulls its message, thereby making it less effective. The public realizes that ads, just as cartoons, do not reflect reality. In the following viewpoint, Clifford G. Christians, Kim B. Rotzoll, and Mark Fackler, professors of communication, write that Americans were raised on mass media and therefore understand how to interpret its messages. Consumers, they say, are not manipulated by advertisements.

As you read, consider the following questions:

1. According to the authors, why are advertisers allowed access to the public?
2. What is the predominant effect of advertising, in the authors' opinion?
3. According to the authors, why are advertising's effects not clearly known?

In order to begin analyzing any aspects of contemporary advertising, it is necessary to understand something of the cultural and economic context within which it functions. The following four premises serve as a useful backdrop for our subsequent description and analysis.

Advertising must be considered in light of cultural expectations. Some forget that we are, in part, a nation founded because of advertising. Daniel Boorstin observes:

> Never was there a more outrageous or more unscrupulous or more ill-informed advertising campaign than that by which the promoters of the American colonies brought settlers here. Brochures published in England in the seventeenth century, some even earlier, were full of hopeful overstatements, half-truths, and downright lies along with some facts which nowadays surely would be the basis of a restraining order from the FTC [Federal Trade Commission]. . . . It would be interesting to speculate how long it might have taken to settle this continent if there had not been such promotion by enterprising advertisers. How has American civilization been shaped by the fact that there was a kind of natural selection here of those people who were willing to believe advertising?

To understand advertising, then, we must be clear about what a given culture expects of it. Some understanding is offered when we grasp the relevant rules of the game. For advertising in this country, the "rules" allow for enterprising businesspeople to pursue their self-interests through various merchandising activities, including advertising. The salesman had always been a prominent part of American culture, honored in fact and fable both for his economic functions and nimble tongue, from the drummers and patent medicine advertisers through the lionization of the often unscrupulous (but always captivating) P.T. Barnum, and the generic flim-flam man.

The Public Is Not Helpless

It is considered appropriate to attempt to persuade. This tells us something concerning our general assumptions about human nature. For why would we permit wanton persuasion to plague a helpless public? Simply because we believe that the public is not helpless, but armed with reason, guile, and a certain savvy about how to make one's way in the market.

If we are sometimes open to persuasion about frivolous products and services, it may be that we have become sufficiently jaded by affluence to let ourselves be seduced by clearly self-interested sources. And it may be, as Theodore Levitt suggests, that advertising serves not only as part of our popular culture but also as an omnipresent source of "alleviating imagery," helping us to mentally compensate for the overall drabness of our lives. We understand advertising only if we understand its culture.

The advertising process has varied intents and effects. How we love to oversimplify. Psychologists say, "The human psychological tendency is toward patterning of experience." And so we say, "Advertising is . . . " and "Advertisements are . . . " and "Advertising does. . . . "

Positive Effects of Advertising

Advertising undoubtedly has many positive features. It is used to promote desirable social aims, like savings and investments, family planning, the purchase of fertiliser to improve agricultural output, etc. It provides the consumer with information about possible patterns of expenditure (in clothing and other personal matters, in house purchase and rental, in travel and holidays, to take obvious examples) and equips him to make choices; this could not be done, or would be done in a much more limited way, without advertising.

Alastair Tempest, *Media Now*, 1985.

Right now, advertisers are attempting to reach and influence individuals for an enormous variety of reasons: here to sell a used power lawn mower through a classified ad; there to induce more patronage of a pizza shop through a hot-air balloon; and yonder an attempt to impart highly technical information about an automated filing system in a journal for office managers. There a detergent minidrama on daytime television. Or a message urging support for the cause of the American Indian. Here the virtues of a high alloy steel in a publication indispensable to metallurgical engineers. Or a campaign on prime time television apparently meant to influence ultimate consumers, but in fact intended to elevate morale among employees and stockholders. And a message asking support of the local police. And so it goes.

Existing Influence

On the receiver end, Joseph Plummer, following years of intensive research, reveals four general levels of potential advertising response: unconscious, immediate perceptual, retention or learning, and behavioral. Then, dealing only with the immediate perceptual level, he finds seven more common responses: entertainment, irritation, familiarity, empathy, confusion, informativeness, and brand reinforcement. The latter response in particular reminds us of the impressive evidence that suggests that the predominant effect of much advertising is not the seduction of the unwashed, but simply the reinforcement of the behavior and judgment of those who already act as some advertisers wish.

Much advertising criticism is directed to television commercials. (Not even the staunchest critic attacks the advertising function in, say, *Harpers.*) Much criticism and defense thus generalizes from specifics to the "All advertising is . . . " syndrome, with a corresponding loss of analytical precision. We understand advertising only if we understand its complexity.

Advertising's actual effects are usually not clearly known. Because of the number of factors involved, for most advertising, most of the time, "no one knows for sure." This explains a great deal. For example:

> •The persistence of the commission system of agency remuneration in which the advertising agency receives a commission (usually 15 percent) on the space and/or time purchased on behalf of the advertiser. If we had any adequate measure of performance, advertisers would compensate their agencies on the basis of proven success. Lacking the needed measure, we rely on a system that rewards the agency not for how well its products (ads) perform, but for how the agency spends its client's money.
>
> •The "me-too" nature of much advertising content. If the business discovers that comparison ads work, we see a rash of such advertisements. If cinema verité is thought to be moving the masses, imitators will proliferate. If fresh-faced young couples strolling in flowered fields are rumored to sell cigarettes, then witness many such pastoral sojourns. Or animation. Or humor. Or folk singers. Or nostalgia. Or candor. Or. . . .
>
> •The lack of true professionalism in the business. Here the wife of the vice-president scuttles an advertising campaign because she doesn't like the look of the female model. There an account executive is browbeaten by an advertising manager about the failure of the agency to come up with some new, creative ideas. Or witness the pomp and circumstance of the Clio awards amid black ties at the Lincoln Center, with giant screens for the embellishment of 30-second color commercials, now transformed from persuasive guesswork into art forms.

Servility and pageantry frequently replace performance, as many accept proxies for the real effect of advertising. We understand advertising only if we understand its uncertainty.

The Ambiguity of Advertising

For all of these reasons, advertising is an ambiguous subject capable of many different interpretations. If one wishes to see advertising as an indispensable element of the free market, one may find what one seeks. If one wishes to see advertising as a sworn enemy of the free market, one may find that as well. Critics and supporters can give to this subject whatever structure they choose. . . .

Advertisements are bits and pieces of reality. *Advertising* is an abstraction from those elements, and from much more. As such, its meaning lies with those who wish to support, to criticize . . . or to understand. We understand advertising only if we understand its ambiguity.

"The tobacco industry still enjoys virtual carte blanche *to sell and promote a lethal product that contains an addictive drug."*

Cigarette Ads Should Be Restricted

Ken Cummins

Since 1971 cigarette advertising has been banned from the airwaves. Many critics of the tobacco industry believe this restriction should apply to all forms of media. Anti-smoking activists would especially like to ban ads directed at children and teenagers. In the following viewpoint, Ken Cummins, a Washington writer, argues that Congress must restrict tobacco companies in advertising a product that causes 340,000 premature deaths per year. If Congress fails to act, Cummins believes that media leaders should voluntarily restrict cigarette ads.

As you read, consider the following questions:

1. According to the author, why was a marketing campaign disputing the link between smoking and cancer started?
2. In the author's opinion, how do tobacco companies target children in their advertising?
3. What does Cummins suggest Congress do to restrict cigarette advertising?

Ken Cummins, "How They Get Away with Murder," *The Washington Monthly,* April 1984. Reprinted with permission from *The Washington Monthly.* Copyright by THE WASHINGTON MONTHLY CO., 1711 Connecticut Ave., NW, Washington, DC 20009. (202) 462-0128.

Today, the tobacco industry may be more on the defensive than ever. Cigarette smoking is being banned from public gathering places, shopping malls, and municipal airports; before the Federal Aviation Administration is a proposal to outlaw smoking on short-haul commercial airflights. Nonsmoking employees are gaining the legal power to curtail or ban smoking in workplaces and an increasing number of corporate and public employers are listing "non-smoking" as a qualification for employment. Meanwhile, periodic reports issued by scientists and the U.S. surgeon general link smoking with even more health problems—most recently, uterine cancer and birthweight deficiencies and illness in children born to women who smoke during their pregnancies.

Perhaps most ominous for the cigarette companies has been the news on the bottom line of their ledger sheets. . . . Cigarette consumption fell for the first time in more than a decade, from 634 billion cigarettes in 1982 to 603 billion in 1983. More alarm bells sounded within the industry when a recent Gallup poll revealed that the proportion of smokers in the population fell from 37 percent in December, 1980 to 29 percent in December, 1982—an all-time low.

An "Open Debate"

The industry's sense of foreboding is perhaps best illustrated by a current advertising campaign by R.J. Reynolds Tobacco Company. The company's advertisements call for an "open debate" on the health effect of smoking, alleging that the link between cigarettes and disease is "not conclusive." The ads have been bitterly denounced by the American Cancer Society, the American Heart Association, and the American Lung Association; the chairman of the latter group's smoking and health committee has linked the call for an "open debate" to "arguing over whether the Second World War occurred."

The ads are right in one respect: it is time for an "open debate." But the topic shouldn't be whether cigarettes are harmful; the evidence that smoking causes at least 340,000 premature deaths a year is as conclusive as it could be. The open debate instead should center on why the tobacco industry still enjoys virtual *carte blanche* to sell and promote a lethal product that contains an addictive drug. (A recent report of the National Institute on Drug Abuse identified nicotine addiction as our leading form of drug dependence.) Compared to the treatment afforded other dangerous substances, the latitude given cigarettes is extraordinary. When pesticides are suspected to cause cancer . . . the substance is often banned outright. When it was discovered that several dozen people had died after taking Eli Lily's Oraflex, the drug was ordered withdrawn from the market and a flood of lawsuits was filed. . . .

[Cigarette] merchandising activities seem to be aimed at children as much as teenagers. Philip Morris allows the distribution and sale of toys and candy cigarettes bearing the familiar trademark of its most popular and successful brand, Marlboro. Last year Kool cigarettes were advertised in more than 3,100 movie houses, many of which were running movies that were rated PG and even G. Action for Children's Television filed a complaint against Brown and Williamson with the Federal Trade Commission after a trailer for Kool cigarettes ran before a showing of "Snow White and the Seven Dwarfs" at a theater in Newton, Massachusetts. The com-

----copyright 1985 by Herblock in The Washington Post.

pany claimed the theater ran the ad by mistake.

Maybe. But there can be no mistake about the young audience that Philip Morris was reaching when it paid an undisclosed amount of money to feature its Marlboro cigarettes in "Superman II." The logo appears some two dozen times, and publicity photos for the movie featured Lois Lane smoking Marlboro cigarettes. If you believe that Philip Morris was really trying to reach the *parents* who took their children to watch the feats of the Man of Steel, you probably also believe that copper bracelets cure arthritis.

This use of subtle advertising techniques has also returned the cigarette industry to the very medium from which it was banned with such fanfare in 1971: television. Last year "Superman II" aired twice during prime-time on ABC, and the Marlboro references were left intact. Cigarette manufacturers have chipped away at the ban in other ways. "When was the last time you watched a football game or baseball game on TV without seeing a Marlboro ad?" comments Matthew Myers, lobbyist for the Coalition on Smoking and Health. "They're right next to the scoreboard in every NFL city." It's not just scoreboards; while winning the 1982 Wimbledon tennis tournament, Martina Navratilova wore the distinctive colors of Kim cigarettes, a British brand. Off the court, Navratilova donned a jacket that prominently displayed the Kim logo.

Who Is Targeted?

Industry spokesmen steadfastly deny that its advertising and promotion efforts target young people. The Tobacco Institute, the cigarette makers' major lobbying arm, currently is running ads that respond with an emphatic "No!" to the question of whether the industry wants teenagers to smoke. "There certainly is the charge that cigarette advertising causes young people to start smoking," says Bill Toohey, spokesman for the Tobacco Institute. "I've asked non-smokers if seeing cigarette ads ever made them want to smoke. I've never yet run into a person who said yes." Toohey says that he started smoking while in college, "and I can't think of any advertising that caused it, either."

Toohey's less than scientific survey not only ignores a fundamental tenet of adolescent psychology—the influence of role models—but a basic fact: most smokers take up the habit in their teens and then can't stop. And given the grim perversities of cigarette marketing—the product causes the early demise of the industry's "best" customers—the industry's future growth obviously depends on getting teenagers and young adults to take up the habit. . . .

All but a handful of newspapers and magazines accept cigarette ads with no restrictions on the amount of space that can be purchased. Very few have any additional requirements about disclosing health effects, and even fewer—*The New Yorker* and the *Christian Science Monitor*, for example—refuse to accept any cigarette ads. Almost none of these publications hold the industry to its own "voluntary guidelines" against advertising that associates smoking with health, beauty, athletic ability, and success. And almost all newspapers accommodate the industry's wish to advertise in those parts of the paper where it feels the impact is greatest, such as the sports section.

Pandering to Advertisers

Such behavior is not just a matter of reluctantly acquiescing in the industry's "right" to advertise what is still a legal product. It's a matter of actively pandering to a major advertiser. Newspaper and magazine publishers could easily adopt their own "voluntary guidelines" that would enforce those of the cigarette makers themselves. But so far, that hasn't happened.

Unhealthy Dependence

Studies dating back to the 1930s provide evidence that the media's dependence on revenue from cigarette advertising has repeatedly led to suppression of discussion of smoking and health matters. . . . The apparent failure of the media to cover issues related to smoking to the extent that their importance should warrant suggests that the public is less knowledgeable about smoking than it ought to be. As a consequence, it seems likely that there are more people who smoke today than there would be in an environment of responsible media coverage. The result is an avoidable excess burden of suffering and premature death.

Kenneth E. Warner, *New England Journal of Medicine*, February 7, 1985.

Compare such eagerness to please with how most newspapers and magazines restrict and even censor ads for pornography, or ads that offend certain ethnic groups or widely accepted standards of taste and accuracy. . . .For example, *Hustler's* Larry Flynt tried to publish a full page advertisement alleging that the CIA had engineered the KAL 007 tragedy. Many newspapers across the country refused to carry the ad, their executives citing "professional responsibility." Offensive as this ad and those for X-rated movies are, they at least have one relative virtue: their influence does not cause people to take up a drug habit that will eventually kill millions of them.

The moral imperative of doing everything reasonable and possible to reduce the staggering toll from cigarette smoking may be felt someday in the executive boardrooms of the nation's publishing media. If that happens, cigarette advertising could be banned entirely. Obviously fearful of that possibility, the tobacco industry has redoubled its efforts in Congress and the media to tell its side of the story. The "open debate" that R.J. Reynolds is calling for on the health issue is unlikely; there's really nothing to debate. Far more likely, R.J. Reynolds and its compatriots will succeed another way: in continuing to stifle the "open debate" that should be raging right now about how to truly deal with America's number one public health problem.

"Tobacco-advertising bans in the five market economies where they exist have not been followed by a decrease in per-capita tobacco consumption."

Cigarette Ads Should Not Be Restricted

J.J. Boddewyn and *The Progressive*

In 1984 the R.J. Reynolds Tobacco Company ran a series of ads disputing the link between smoking and cancer. Anti-smoking groups were enraged but tobacco companies asserted their Constitutional right to air their opinions. Tobacco lobbyists said that the First Amendment guarantees their right to advertise. In Part I of the following two-part viewpoint, J.J. Boddewyn, the editor of a Children's Research Unit study on juvenile smoking, states that cigarette ad bans imposed on five countries did not reduce smoking. In Part II an editorial from *The Progressive* states that though smoking causes harm, the US government has no right to restrict free speech.

As you read, consider the following questions:

1. According to the statistics given by Boddewyn, what resulted from the ban on tobacco advertisements in other countries?
2. On what grounds does *The Progressive* defend cigarette advertisements?

J.J. Boddewyn, "Smoking Ads Don't Get People Hooked," *The Wall Street Journal*, October 21, 1986. Reprinted with permission.
The Progressive, "Smoke Signals, Too, Are a Form of Free Speech," September 1986. Copyright © 1986, The Progressive, Inc. Reprinted by permission from The Progressive, Madison, WI 53703.

Hearings in the 99th Congress on Rep. Mike Synar's "Health Protection Act of 1986" were a prelude to a more serious move . . . to ban all forms of tobacco advertising. It is ill-advised.

Supporters of this bill used a four-part argument: (1) Smoking is bad for your health and that of others; (2) advertising plays a crucial role in making people start and continue smoking— particularly, the very young; (3) Supreme Court decisions allow the state to do pretty much anything it wants in controlling advertising ("commercial speech"), and, therefore, (4) a ban on all forms of tobacco advertising is appropriate. I leave it to others to debate the health and legal issues. However, based on research with which I have been associated, I strongly question the role ascribed to advertising and the efficacy imputed to an advertising ban.

Bans Do Not Stop Smoking

First, tobacco-advertising bans in the five market economies where they exist have not been followed by a decrease in per-capita tobacco consumption. In Italy, such consumption is up by 68% after a 22-year ban; in Iceland, by 13% after 13 years; in Singapore, by 12% after 14 years; in Norway, by 6% after nine years, and in Finland, by 3% after six years. Recent statistics are all up, too. On the other hand, cigarette sales decreased by 26% between 1974 and 1983, in the United Kingdom where there is no ban but restrictions similar to those in the U.S. These numbers are generally based on government statistics, and hard to refute.

Advertising bans also hamper the dissemination of information about new tobacco products with lower tar and nicotine, better filters and similar improvements. In ban countries such as Finland and Norway, people smoke fewer cigarettes containing lower tar than they do in Sweden, where such a ban does not exist.

Ads Do Not Recruit

Does advertising make the young start smoking? To answer that question, we depend on survey results that are less reliable than the government statistics used in the advertising-ban studies. Besides, many surveys of juvenile smoking have used written questionnaires administered in school settings with authoritarian and anti-smoking atmospheres. A 1984-1986 study by the London-based Children's Research Unit tried to avoid these problems by using personal interviews conducted at home in four countries, besides incorporating comparable survey data collected for the British government. This five-nation study provides three major findings.

Advertising was mentioned as the most important reason for why they started smoking by not more than 1% of the seven-to-15 year-old juveniles interviewed. On the other hand, the influence of parents, siblings and friends came out as the overwhelming factor associated with smoking initiation. This is hardly a novel finding since practically all U.S. and foreign studies have reached the same conclusion. What is new, however, is that the non-influence of advertising on juvenile smoking initiation was identical in all five countries, irrespective of whether there was an advertising ban (in Norway), major advertising restrictions (in Australia and the United Kingdom) or minor advertising controls (in Hong Kong and Spain).

Fighting the Censor's Axe

Ads don't cause people to smoke or recklessly consume alcohol. At most, they only cause consumers to switch brands. Bans or restrictions would thus do nothing to curb alleged abuses. . . .

Ad bans would deprive consumers of important information. Cigarette ads often contain, for example, information on tar and nicotine, which some consumers use to switch brands.

Finally, if cigarette ads are to be banned, what's to stop the censor's axe from falling on many other products—such as ads for meat or eggs (with high cholesterol levels) or automobiles (in which up to 50,000 Americans die every year)?

Tracy Westen, *Media & Values*, Fall 1986.

For that matter, the percentage of regular smokers among youngsters aged seven to 15 is two times higher in Norway (where there is a ban) than among Australian and Spanish juvenile smokers, and 10 times higher than the percentage of smoking youngsters in Hong Kong. Clearly, other variables—personal, social, cultural and educational—are at work.

No Strong Links

Does advertising encourage young people to continue smoking by affirming the legitimacy of the practice? We don't quite know the answer to that question because it is practically impossible to disentangle the impact of advertising from that of other relevant factors. For that matter, we know very little about why anybody is a regular smoker, a nonsmoker or a former smoker: Only a few hundred psychological or sociological studies bearing on that question exist, compared with more than 50,000 on the effects of smoking on health. It is apparent that as a child grows older, adult aspirations and identification with adults increase, the child's peer group widens and includes people with a greater variety of behavior patterns, the child's mobility and spending power increase, and the age for legal purchase of the product approaches.

In any case, the amount of advertising exposure is low compared with the numerous daily sightings of cigarettes, packages and smoking situations. Besides, for every ad showing young-adult smokers living the good life and having clean fun, there are many anti-smoking, public-service messages, school lectures, articles and books, pack warnings, nonsmoking signs and other restrictions in public and private places as well as frowns and rebukes from anti-smokers. Their respective impact is largely unknown, however.

Still, we do know that smoking prevalence is as high or higher among 15-year-olds in Norway where there has been a ban on tobacco advertising since 1975, compared with non-ban countries. This evidence strongly suggests that: (1) Tobacco-advertising bans are not effective in reducing overall consumption, and (2) advertising plays an insignificant role in the initiation of smoking by the young and even in its continuation.

A Non-Solution

It is tempting for the U.S. Congress to promote a tobacco-advertising ban because of its highly symbolic value. To its proponents, such a ban would be a sign that smoking is no longer considered socially acceptable. However, before engaging in another "noble experiment" in social engineering, akin to the Prohibition Amendment, which lasted about as long as has the recent experience with tobacco-advertising bans in five countries, it is worth pondering whether a good end justifies a poor means—a non-solution, in fact.

The Synar bill probably will be reintroduced . . . and Rep. Henry Waxman (D., Calif.) . . . is likely to advance his own bill limiting tobacco advertisements to "tombstone ads"' restricted to the reproduction of the logo, the Surgeon General's warnings, and tax and nicotine contents—possibly coupled with other promotion curbs. This attempt at eliminating the "imagery" associated with tobacco advertising may gather greater support than a total ban, but its scientific rationale is as feeble as that of the Synar bill. But then, advertising always provides an easy target when regulators look for a scapegoat.

II

Should R.J. Reynolds, the tobacco company, be allowed to place advertisements in major newspapers challenging the scientific validity of studies that have implicated cigarette smoking in a higher incidence of cardiovascular disease? The Federal Trade Commission (FTC) has ruled that such ads should be banned because they mislead and defraud consumers. But the FTC's position raises questions that should trouble even those who believe— as we do—that tobacco producers and distributors are merchants of death.

206

The FTC's attempts to suppress the R.J. Reynolds ad relies on the notion that "commercial speech" is not entitled to the full protection of the First Amendment. Certainly the FTC is right when it insists that some special constraints must be imposed on certain forms of commercial speech. The manufacturer or vendor who mislabels products by concealing or misrepresenting ingredients can pose an immediate danger to the public. Such requirements as warning labels on hazardous substances (including cigarettes) or accurate ingredient information give consumers the data they need to make safe, rational choices in the marketplace.

Wayne Stayskal. Reprinted by permission: Tribune Media Services.

But does this mean that R.J. Reynolds has no right to contest the scientific consensus on which the smoking warning is based? May the Government insist that its scientific findings are the last word—beyond challenge or contradiction? Is "commercial speech" to be stripped of First Amendment protection even when the speech at issue addresses fundamental questions of public policy—as did the R.J. Reynolds ad banned by the FTC? Such advertisements may, in fact, serve a commercial end, inducing a few more individuals to consider smoking. But the proper Government response is to marshal and propagate the most effective response in opposition to the tobacco industry's arguments—not to ban publication of those arguments.

The FTC's approach is more likely to undermine the credibility of scientific research and of government than of the tobacco companies. Government-sanctioned science is and ought to be alien to the American experience. It smacks of the Stalinist suppression of all genetic science that did not conform to the exotic theories of Trofim Lysenko.

Choosing Our Community

Such vast multinational comglomerates as R.J. Reynolds wield immense power, including the power to expound their views to the public by buying great quantities of print space and broadcast time. They can—and do—inflict grave injury on immense numbers of consumers. But the answer is not to be found in an arbitrary Government decision to curtail the freedom of speech of these corporate giants. Instead, we should mount a serious effort to limit their economic power and to provide wider media access to the rest of us.

The real issue here is what kind of political community we will have—one where a Government agency determines the range of views we may hold and express, or one where the broadest exchange of views is seen as a positive virtue in its own right and as a safeguard against the imposition of a hasty and unjustified consensus.

"We view advertising reforms . . . as one facet of a comprehensive program to re-define the role of alcohol in our society."

A Ban on Alcohol Ads Would Aid Society

Michael F. Jacobson

Alcohol abuse costs Americans billions of dollars and thousands of lives each year. No one promotes alcohol abuse. However, critics of the alcohol industry believe it is unconscionable for alcohol manufacturers to advertise such a destructive product. The following viewpoint is a speech addressed to the Senate Subcommittee on Alcoholism and Drug Abuse. In it, Michael F. Jacobson, executive director of the Center for Science in the Public Interest, argues that alcohol ads should be banned, or opposing views given equal time, because they encourage young people to drink and current drinkers to consume more.

As you read, consider the following questions:

1. According to Jacobson, how do alcohol ads encourage young people to drink?
2. Does Jacobson believe alcohol ads cause consumers to switch brands, or do they increase consumption?
3. Does the author believe public support exists for reforms in alcohol advertising? Why or why not?

Michael F. Jacobson, testimony before the Subcommittee on Alcoholism and Drug Abuse, Senate Committee on Labor and Human Resources, February 6, 1985. Reprinted with the author's permission.

The issue being addressed is alcohol advertising. But the underlying issue is really the devastation related to alcohol in homes, schools, and businesses in every corner of America. While our society has never been, and probably never will be, totally free of alcohol problems, it is appropriate to ask . . . whether and how the $750 million a year worth of radio and television commercials for beer and wine contribute to the estimated 100,000-plus lives lost each year and the $120 billion in economic costs to our nation.

Kids grow up in a sea of advertising. They start seeing beer and wine commercials—and sometimes start singing the jingles—at the age of 3 or 4. They will see and hear thousands of commercials exhorting them to drink even before they reach the legal drinking age. . . .

Violating the Codes

Despite industry's claims that ads are not targeted at heavy drinkers or youths, the Coors Lite ad tells viewers to drink ''beer after beer and don't hold back . . . turn it loose.'' Harvey's Bristol Cream sherry teaches viewers to switch from traditional glasses to giant tumblers. Anheuser-Busch uses actor-athletes to show viewers that Bud Lite will bring out their best. The Wild Irish Rose wine ad, which depicts a Michael Jackson look-alike and break-dancing along with rock music, seems to be targeting grade school and high school kids. Ads like these violate the voluntary, and toothless, advertising codes of producers and broadcasters. Ads on radio are often disguised as popular music so they blend right in with the programming. Objective minds can hardly deny that the overall effect of the ads is to glamorize alcohol and foster the notion that drinking is the key to achieving personal goals.

While we are troubled by the content of certain ads, we're more concerned about their machine gun-like frequency and the virtual absence on the public airwaves of honest, complete, persuasive information about alcohol. The relative absence of public service announcements that inform both youths and adults that you can be a success and have friends without drinking a six-pack of beer is disgraceful. Wouldn't it be terrific, if sports stars, famous actresses, and others helped popularize a lifestyle in which alcohol wasn't a necessity, but simply one choice among many beverages.

Alcohol researchers generally believe that alcohol problems rise in rough proportion to consumption. Also, it is evident that when you spend billions of advertising dollars promoting a group of products—like beer and wine—consumption of those products will rise . . . and, in fact, alcohol consumption has increased by almost 50 percent per capita since 1960. When it comes to alcohol, however, it is comic to hear the producers and broadcasters argue that ads do not increase consumption, only switch people from one brand to another. As a writer in "Advertising Age" observed, "A strange world it is, in which people spending millions on advertising must do their best to prove that advertising doesn't do very much!"

Boosting Sales

In fact, there is ample evidence to support the common sense view that billion dollar advertising assaults boost sales.

- First, . . . marketing executives readily acknowledge that they want to maximize sales, partly through advertising. As one major wine advertiser said, "Today we consider any liquid at all our competitor. We're positioning ourselves like a soft drink."
- Government-sponsored studies . . . demonstrate a convincing association between advertising and consumption.
- Also, Americans are . . . participating in an illuminating natural experiment. Beer and wine companies spend enormous sums on broadcast ads. Liquor companies, to their credit, spend nothing. Look at sales over the past decade: beer and wine sales increased steadily until leveling off in the past year or two, while liquor sales are down in nine of the past ten years.

Bill Garner for *The Washington Times*. Reprinted with permission.

To try to reduce the pressure to drink, a coalition of citizens' groups in 1982 wrote to all major alcohol producers in the U.S., asking that they voluntarily reform their marketing practices. We did not hear from a single company.

The next year, a coalition of citizens groups petitioned the Federal Trade Commission to implement major reforms of alcohol advertising. Fifteen months later, we still [had] not received a reply.

Therefore, in 1984 more than two dozen national citizens groups, and literally hundreds of state and local ones . . . mounted a national grassroots petition campaign called "Project SMART" to show Congress that the public wants action. We are seeking one million signatures in support of *either* a ban on beer and wine commercials, *or* an equal time requirement.

Public Support for Ban

The public has shown tremendous support for doing something about alcohol commercials: over 700,000 people have already signed the SMART petition, and a . . . public opinion survey showed the public divided almost evenly on whether beer and wine commercials should be outlawed. We believe that an overwhelming majority of the public supports an equal-time rule.

This support for a ban or equal time is consistent with what First Amendment authorities, like Stanford Law Professor Marc Franklin, have determined is a legitimate area for congressional action.

I should add, in conclusion, that we view advertising reforms not as a panacea, but as one facet of a comprehensive program to re-define the role of alcohol in our society. Sweden has implemented just such a program, and that nation's alcohol consumption and problem drinking have been declining significantly.

"Singling out advertising as a whipping boy for the [alcohol] problem doesn't . . . address society's main concern: the misuse of alcohol."

A Ban on Alcohol Ads Would Not Aid Society

Edward O. Fritts

Spokespersons for the alcohol industry agree that a serious alcohol problem exists in the US. In their opinion, however, banning alcohol ads would not decrease alcohol abuse, but would only weaken the First Amendment. In the following viewpoint, Edward O. Fritts, president of the National Association of Broadcasters, writes that advertising does not create alcohol abuse. He also states that a ban on alcohol ads would cripple radio and television stations' ability to cover sporting events.

As you read, consider the following questions:

1. The author states that alcohol ads do not promote over-indulgence. What then do they promote?
2. In the author's opinion, why would censoring alcohol ads be illogical?
3. According to Fritts, how much revenue does alcohol advertising generate?

Edward O. Fritts, "Broadcasters: Can't Treat a Social Ill with Censorship," *Los Angeles Times*, March 10, 1985. Reprinted with the author's permission.

A prohibitionist movement is afoot to remove beer and wine ads from the airwaves. The premise is that a ban on such ads will work wonders in solving the serious problem of alcohol abuse in our nation.

Obviously, alcohol abuse has been around long before radio and TV. It is a national tragedy of great concern to all. Singling out advertising as a whipping boy for the problem doesn't make sense and doesn't address society's concern: the misuse of alcohol.

The Influence of Ads

Examine the facts. We are talking about alcohol abuse—not alcohol use.

- Studies indicate that 35% of Americans are teetotalers; 65% drink, and of those 10% are heavy drinkers including problem drinkers.

- Common sense tells us that advertising on radio and TV doesn't create an alcoholic. Drinking behavior is influenced by a variety of psychological and physiological factors, the most important being family example, followed by peer pressure.

- There is not one recognized study linking broadcast advertising of beer and wine with overindulgence. What advertising does is play a fundamental role in influencing which brand a beer or wine drinker chooses to buy. The fact is, if Miller can persuade 1% of the beer-drinking public to shift to its brand, that represents nearly $400 million at the retail level.

- Cigarette advertising was taken off the air in 1971. Yet the rate of smoking by young people who have never seen nor heard a broadcast cigarette ad remains exceedingly high despite the Surgeon General's and subsequent reports. An important distinction remains: One cigarette is harmful to your health, one drink is not.

- Other nations, including the Soviet Union, Sweden, Norway and Finland, do not allow broadcast alcohol advertising, and yet they have considerably higher rates of alcohol misuse than the United States.

The move to ban such ads in the United States neglects the issue and deflects energies away from productively dealing with alcohol abuse.

Public Service Announcements

Broadcasters have taken up the challenge. In communities across the country, through public service announcements, public affairs programming, newscasts and cooperative community efforts, the consciousness of the people is being raised. Once again, we seek to curb abuse, not use.

Long before the issue of the ban was raised, the National Assn. of Broadcasters launched a massive drunk driving/alcohol misuse and drug abuse campaign. This voluntary effort is now under way, and many radio and TV stations across the country are participating. . . . Our role in dealing with these problems is to make the public aware, to work with other interested groups to publicize and augment their work.

As journalists, it is particularly perplexing to us to have to seriously consider censorship as a means of dealing with a social ill. In essence, this is what the ban proposes. It has focused on lawful products—beer and wine—seeking to eliminate ads for those products from the airwaves in an effort to cure alcohol abuse. The logic is mystifying. How about a ban on automobile advertisements to stop car crashes? Or a ban on milk and butter ads to stop the problem of high cholesterol?

A Free Society

The coalition [Project SMART—Stop Marketing Alcohol on Radio and Television] gripes that radio and TV ads glamorize drinking. No doubt they do; ads wouldn't sell much beer by convincing people it's disgusting.

But in a free society, why should it be illegal for sellers to "glamorize" legal products? Anyone who disagrees is perfectly free to propagandize against it. To silence your opponents is to admit the weakness of your case.

The coalition worries that children may be unduly influenced by these ads. Well, that's why there are laws against selling alcohol to minors. The gullibility of children is no ground for putting a straitjacket on adults. Among the pubescent, tobacco-chewing ballplayers are the best publicity chewing tobacco could get. Should we forbid telecasts showing any player with a bulge in his cheek?

Stephen Chapman, *The Washington Times*, January 29, 1985.

Advocates of the ban claim that beer and wine spots are poisoning the minds of our young people who watch them, particularly during sporting events. Nielsen, the accepted broadcast rating service, finds that less than 3% of teens are in the sports audience. Further, the advocates say that the use of athletes in advertising glamorizes and entices youth to drink—and drink hard. But Marvelous Marv Throneberry, Bob Uecker or Bernie (Boom Boom) Geoffrion are hardly a 16-year-old's role model. These ads are designed to appeal to middle-aged beer drinkers who like robust taste but must count calories. One can only wonder if the ban advocates also disapprove of the Clydesdales trotting through the countryside at Christmas or the farmers in the field clapping for the lone Olympic Torch bearer.

There is yet another side effect to this curious attempt by neo-prohibition, and it is one that will be felt at the local level by many Americans. It is the bottom line. Beer and wine advertising accounts for 4% to 5% of TV revenues and 12% of radio's. The average radio station's annual profit is 7.29%. It doesn't take a mathematical wizard to determine the consequences.

A ban on beer and wine advertising will have an impact, all right. It will threaten the networks' ability to carry sporting events. It will make some people feel they have done something, anything, about the problem at hand. It will satisfy those who preach against "demon rum."

What it will not do is solve the problem of alcohol abuse.

"Playing with war toys legitimizes and makes violent behavior acceptable."

Advertising of War Toys Should Be Regulated

National Coalition on Television Violence

Critics of the war toy industry believe that super-hero cartoons and their corresponding advertisements teach children that violence is acceptable social behavior. They also argue that young children cannot distinguish between violent cartoons and the advertisements they spawn. The following viewpoint is taken from a press release from the National Coalition on Television Violence [NCTV]. In it, the NCTV writes that war toys and their advertisements have a harmful effect on children and should therefore be regulated. The NCTV also urges parents to replace violent toys with nonviolent toys.

As you read, consider the following questions:

1. According to Arnold Goldstein, what happens when children become desensitized to violence?
2. In Thomas Radecki's opinion, how should violent advertising be countered?
3. Why does Radecki fear the impact of war toys and violent advertising on children?

National Coalition on Television Violence press release, "War Cartoons and War Toys Grow in Number," November 24, 1986. Reprinted with permission.

The sales of war toys has increased by 700% since 1982, including a 22% increase in the first half of [1986]. 11 of the 20 best selling toys in America have themes of violence. Realistic war toys, machine guns, and infrared combat gun sets are selling fast. G.I. Joe is the #1 best selling toy in America and Rambo weapons have hit the toy shelves. . . .

Arnold Goldstein, Ph.D., director of the Center for Research on Aggression at the University of Syracuse says, "The playing with war toys legitimizes and makes violent behavior acceptable. It desensitizes children to the dangers and harm of violent behavior and increases the chance that they will resort to violent behavior. Probably only a small number will commit heavy duty violence, but a large number get desensitized and will pick up some harmful behaviors. The degree that youngsters are learning to take pleasure from aggression decreases their ability to learn empathy, negotiation, and cooperation. I would recommend that parents not allow violent toys in their homes, but purchase nonviolent toys and games."

Leonard Eron, Ph.D., University of Illinois researcher who has done long-term studies on the impact of TV violence on children in the U.S. and five foreign countries says, "I am sure violent toys and their cartoons have harmful effects on a wide variety of children. They rehearse at home beating up on people, killing them. The more they rehearse, the more likely they are to store up these patterns of behavior. I don't think that there is any doubt that violent entertainment is having a harmful effect on our society and on our world."

Regulate War Toys

Civic, church, peace, and health groups are demonstrating in cities like San Antonio and Minneapolis, Hartford and San Diego. They say that children and their parents have a right and need to know that these toys have harmful effects. They are handing out flyers, sticking warning labels on military toys and even in some cases getting arrested in the process. They say that there is an urgent need for legislation to get a warning to children and their parents that playing with toy weapons and having fun with fantasies of killing is a bad idea. The groups would like to see legislation banning the use of cartoons to sell toys of violence to children. They support the Children's Television Education Act, a bill which would require that every TV station carry at least one hour of positive children's programming each day. The legislation has been stalled in congress due to industry opposition.

Doug Thomson, president of the Toy Manufacturers of America, in a meeting with citizen groups said that he opposes the idea of a panel of toy industry officials investigating the research evidence and determining what should be done. He also opposes any governmental hearings, any warnings on television, and any public funding of further research into the harmful effects of violent toys. . . .

Protecting America's Children

NCTV's [Thomas] Radecki says, "It is a tragedy that, at least until now, our government has cooperated in helping to make the situation still worse. . . .

"When the U.S. Food and Drug Administration requires only two studies to label a medication as effective, I think it is a terrible mistake that 39 studies finding harmful effects on children are ignored. Thanks to legislation quickly enacted [in 1985], a retail store that sells one counterfeit toy can be fined $1,000,000. If the store is caught selling a counterfeit toy a second time, it can be fined $5,000,000 with the owner sent to prison for up to 15 years! Our government plays real hardball when it comes to protecting the profits of the toy industry, but when it comes to protecting the mental health of America's children, nothing is done. In a democracy, it is the responsibility of government to assure that defective and dangerous merchandise is appropriately labelled. Advertising and selling violence to children, if permitted, should be balanced by counter-advertisements getting the message of the Surgeon General out to our children. They need to know that the Surgeon General has determined that a diet of violent entertain-

Danziger in The Christian Science Monitor © 1986 TCSPS.

ment has harmful effects on your mental, and physical well-being."

According to Robert Gould, M.D., a practicing psychiatrist at the New York Medical College and NCTV boardmember, the more children are exposed to violent cartoons, TV or toys, the more they accept it as a way of life. It becomes a part of them, of their personalities. He says that many people will be affected in small ways that they could never notice. For others, it becomes something they may emulate in later life with a gun or knife, although they may not be able to explain how it came about.

Real Life Violence

Radecki reports two cases from his own psychiatric practice. [In 1986] he participated in the murder trial of a 15-year-old Orlando, Florida boy, one of a group of adolescents who had been repeatedly playing war together. They murdered a convenience store clerk in order to get money to help set up their own military camp. He says the boy he examined was very strongly influenced by violent and war entertainment.

Radecki also describes a 14-year-old boy who repeatedly played Rambo in war games with his friends. The boy later saw the *Rambo, First Blood II* movie several times in a row. The youth went to enlist in the military but was turned down because of age. He became very frustrated, got in an argument with his mother, tried to kill himself and had to be admitted to the hospital. He was wearing a Rambo headband and had a U.S. flag draped from his waist. According to Radecki, the youth said over and over, "I just wanted to kill communists and make my parents proud."

Radecki said, "These examples are just the tip of the iceberg and are exceptional cases. However, I am just one of 30,000 psychiatrists so there must be a lot more cases out there. But, what I am really worried about is what the impact is on the next generation of America's leaders. Whether we like to admit it or not, America's first TV generation has grown up to be the most violent generation in our history, murdering each other 250% more often per capita, raping women 500% more and assaulting each other 600% more per capita than our parents' generation. The second TV generation is growing up on much stronger stuff."

*"There is absolutely no evidence, academic or
. . . practical, that playing with soldiers has any
bad influence on later behavior."*

Advertising of War Toys Should Not Be Regulated

Douglas Thomson

Millions of children have grown up pretending they were Davy
Crockett, the Lone Ranger, or GI Joe. Toy company executives say
children have fantasized about war from the beginning of history
without harm to society. They argue that if war toys, or their advertisements, were harmful, parents would ignore them. In the
following viewpoint Douglas Thomson, president of the Toy
Manufacturers of America, writes that war toys do not have a
detrimental effect on children. He believes a ban on advertising
would hinder the freemarket system and not be effective in stop-
ping children from playing war games.

As you read, consider the following questions:

1. Why does the author argue that criticism of war toys will
   change nothing?
2. According to Thomson, how does the free enterprise
   system regulate harmful products?
3. Thomson does not believe that war toys cause violent
   behavior. In his opinion, what does?

Douglas Thomson, "War Toys, Yes," *Detroit Free Press*, November 23, 1986. Copyright
1986, Detroit Free Press.

Children have long played with toy soldiers and miniature cannons.

The first toy I ever bought with my own money was a toy George Washington, resplendent on his white horse, in the uniform of the Continental Army, sword in hand.

I played by the hour with World War I soldiers with horses, caissons and motorcycles, because that was a simulation of what my father's generation was all about.

Later I graduated to Dick Tracy, the Lone Ranger, the Green Hornet and the Shadow.

My son, in turn, was G.I. Joe at Halloween, Davy Crockett (with coonskin cap and long rifle) at nursery school graduation, Johnny West with appropriate six shooter. Millions of adults are fascinated with Patton, remember Eisenhower with great fondness, turn out for parades, hope their youngsters go to a military academy (applications are way up) and look with admiration at the brilliant and brave astronauts.

Undue Criticism

So why the sudden spate of development specialists, syndicated columnists and so-called advocates who have turned their criticisms on the toy industry for producing cap pistols, action figures, space warriors, Jeeps and combat aircraft models?

I say these people speak for themselves, not necessarily for children. They have found a cause, and not a difficult cause, but one that looks good in print and makes for good argument.

But they have little chance of changing things. Let me suggest why:

First, children emulate adults, who they think live interesting, exciting lives. They want the same music, dance, cars, and action as big brother and sister, as mother and dad—or as the TV, movie and magazine adults. We all did as children. Remember when you wanted to be a policeman, fireman, FBI agent, nurse, doctor, soldier, famous scientist? Remember when you couldn't wait to drive a car?

Many of our heroes of both fiction and real life are armed: detectives, Bengal Lancers, Gary Cooper, John Kennedy as a PT boat commander, Robert Louis Stevenson's characters, Prince Valliant, Robin Hood.

Children dress up and pretend, with arms if they fit the game. They are part of their fantasy, their growing up—as life has been since early man gave his son a pretend weapon.

Are children who play with toy weapons more or less violent? We often get both sides of every question from child development specialists. Milk is good—or it's bad. Thumb sucking is OK—but maybe not.

I remember when sneakers were proclaimed bad for children's

feet, but they sure are comfortable and practical. I like the practical side; I talk to parents all over the country and find them eminently intelligent and down to earth. They know that what is good for one child may be bad for another—and only mother and dad can tell. Each family must make judgments about eating habits, studying times, TV and radio use, dress codes, manners, and so on, with some truly difficult issues.

It is perplexing that critics have put so much time and attention on toys when the terrible large issues need all the focus possible: drugs, real guns, intellectual skills, crime and moral judgments, to name a few.

Freedom of Choice

I don't believe there are any occult toys on the market. As for violent toys, we've looked at the data, and we've never seen a definitive study that says playing with cap pistols ever did any harm to a child.

Most people today, particularly males, grew up playing with some sort of simulated weapon, and most of them are not violent, unhappy or murderous. We respond to what customers want . . . that's mom and dad. The gut issue is that people who don't like these toys can buy others.

Douglas Thomson, *El Paso Times*, May 18, 1986.

My second point is that this great American system of free enterprise means that the products that critics harp on would not exist if parents did not buy them. No retailer or manufacturer would be involved in making such toys if sales did not tell; the marketplace speaks swiftly and sometimes brutally.

G.I. Joe Halloween costumes are extremely popular because young boys and their parents think they are fun for dressing up. Star Wars, Masters of the Universe and robots sell big because children want them and parents buy them.

Parents will not buy what is tasteless or dangerous for their children. I, for instance, would not purchase a BB gun for my son, because of the area in which we live.

Common Sense

My last point has to do with the effects of playing with cap pistols, Jeeps, tanks and toy soldiers. Let's apply some good old-fashioned horse sense. I judge that virtually every reader . . . at one time or another, as a child, played cowboys and Indians, cops and robbers, or even war.

They have read books, seen movies and watched TV programs about war and injury, death and victory and defeat. They have learned from these experiences, questioned their meaning, and formed values. The vast majority of the American public are decent, honest, non-violent citizens.

There is absolutely no evidence, academic or, most important, practical, that playing with soldiers has any bad influence on later behavior. Violent teenagers and adults are products of far deeper problems of our society. I always found that discussing weapons, war and adventure with my son was an opportunity to establish truth and values to help him face the real world.

Intellectual Snobs

When I meet with the critics of toy weapons, I invariably ask if they played with toys like cap pistols when they were children. They almost always answer affirmatively and say they didn't become violent adults for some reason, and usually cite education.

They aren't worried about their children—or mine. Only about the children of those poor people out there who don't know any better. I say that's hogwash. It's intellectual snobbery.

I have great confidence in American parents. If they don't want the children to see TV programs, the set will be turned off. If they don't like the toys, they will refuse to buy them. And they will soon disappear from toy shelves.

Distinguishing Between Fact and Opinion

This activity is designed to help develop the basic reading and thinking skill of distinguishing between fact and opinion. Consider the following statement as an example: "In 1983, cigarette consumption fell for the first time in more than a decade." This statement is a fact that can be confirmed by comparing the data on smoking over a ten-year period. But consider a statement which links cigarette advertising to recruiting young smokers. "Cigarette merchandising is aimed at children as well as their parents." Such a statement conveys the author's opinion. Readers who oppose cigarette smoking may agree but others would not.

When studying controversial issues it is important that one be able to distinguish between statements of fact and statements of opinion. It is also important to recognize that not all statements of fact are true. They may appear to be true but some are based on inaccurate or false information. For this activity, however, we are concerned with understanding the difference between those statements which appear to be factual and those which appear to be based primarily on opinion.

The following statements are taken from the viewpoints in this chapter. Consider each statement carefully. *Mark O for any statement you believe is an opinion or interpretation of facts. Mark F for any statement you believe is a fact.*

If you are doing this activity as a member of a class or group, compare your answers with those of other class or group members. Be able to defend your answers. You may discover that others will come to different conclusions than you. Listening to the reasons others present for their answers may give you valuable insights in distinguishing between fact and opinion.

$$O = opinion$$
$$F = fact$$

1. Advertising picks up most of the costs of newspapers and magazines and all the costs of radio and television.

2. Over and above any particular product, they (commercials) sell an entire way of life, a way of experiencing social reality that is compatible with the needs of a mass-production, mass-consumption, capitalistic society.

3. Most consumers, if questioned on the matter, would agree that many commercials are exaggerated, unrealistic, and even untrue.

4. Much advertising criticism is directed toward television commercials.

5. The overall effect of alcohol ads is to glamorize alcohol and foster the notion that drinking is the key to achieving personal goals.

6. I am sure violent toys and their cartoons have harmful effects on a wide variety of children.

7. Advertisements are bits and pieces of reality.

8. In the American free enterprise system, toys that critics harp on would not exist if parents did not buy them.

9. Advertising's actual effects are hard to prove.

10. Nonsmoking employees are gaining the legal power to ban smoking in workplaces.

11. An increasing number of employers are listing "nonsmoking" as a qualification for employment.

12. The evidence that smoking causes at least 340,000 premature deaths a year is as conclusive as it could be.

13. The sales of war-related toys has increased by 700 percent since 1982.

14. Advertising plays an insignificant role in the initiation of smoking by the young.

15. Tobacco-advertising bans have not been followed by a decrease in per-capita tobacco consumption.

16. There is absolutely no evidence that playing with toy soldiers has any bad influence on later behavior.

17. Other nations do not allow broadcast alcohol advertising, and yet they have considerably higher rates of alcohol abuse than the US.

Periodical Bibliography

The following articles have been selected to supplement the diverse views expressed in this chapter.

Dennis M. Adams and Mary Fuchs	"The Video Media and Cultural Misunderstanding," *USA Today*, November 1986.
C.C. Carter	"Sudsless Sports?" *Fortune*, January 21, 1985.
Glamour	"This Is What You Thought: 88% Say TV Violence Makes Kids Violent," February 1987.
Margot Hornblower	"In the Media Generation, the Ads Have To Be Less Filling," *The Washington Post National Weekly Edition*, June 16, 1986.
John Kavanaugh	"Idols of the Marketplace," *Media & Values*, Fall 1986.
Ann Lallande	"Tobacco, Know Thy Enemies," *Marketing & Media*, October 1986.
Leil Lowndes	"Junk Television," *The World & I*, April 1987.
NCTV News	Newsletter of the National Coalition on Television Violence. Any issue. Available from PO Box 2157, Champaign, IL 61820.
Jonathan Rowe	"Gauging the Impact of Advertising," *The Christian Science Monitor*, January 28, 1987.
Rosalind Silver	"Mighty Messages Make Marketing Memorable," *Media & Values*, Fall 1986.
Harold Smith	"A Colossal Cover-Up," *Christianity Today*, December 12, 1986.
Elizabeth Stark	"Kids' TV: Fewer Words from Our Sponsors," *Psychology Today*, July 1985.
Clifford Williams	"Direct Attack on the First Amendment," *engage/social action*, January 1985.
Daniel B. Wood	"High-Tech War Toys Storm TV and Theater," *The Christian Science Monitor*, February 19, 1987.
Melvin L. Wulf	"Advertising Pleads the First," *Commonweal*, February 13, 1987.

Organizations To Contact

The editors have compiled the following list of organizations which are concerned with the issues debated in this book. All of them have publications available for interested readers. The descriptions are derived from materials provided by the organizations themselves.

Accuracy in Media (AIM)
1275 K St. NW, Suite 1150
Washington, DC 20005
(202) 371-6710

This group is a conservative news media watchdog organization. It researches public complaints on errors of fact made by the news media. It requests that the errors be corrected publicly. It publishes *AIM Report*, bimonthly and a weekly syndicated newspaper column.

Action for Children's Television (ACT)
46 Austin St.
Newtonville, MA 02160
(617) 876-6620

The group's purposes are "to encourage and support quality programming for children, to eliminate commercialism from children's programs, and to require a reasonable amount of programming each week designed for children of different ages." They have published *The ACT Guide to Children's Television: How To Treat TV with TLC*, and *New Views and Viewing/ACT TV Time Chart*. They also publish a news magazine and books.

Alternative Information Network (AIN)
PO Box 7279-A
Austin, TX 78713
(512) 453-4894

The goal of the Network is to promote public access to alternative media, which includes the resources of public interest groups and groups advocating social change. It publishes *Alternative Views Program Catalog*.

American Advertising Federation (AAF)
1400 K St. NW, Suite 1000
Washington, DC 20005
(202) 898-0089

The group strives "to promote a better understanding of advertising through government relations, public relations, and advertising education in order to further an effective program of advertising self-regulation." Publications include the monthly *Communicator*, the monthly *Washington Report*, and the quarterly *American Advertising Magazine*.

American Cancer Society
90 Park Ave.
New York, NY 10016
(212) 736-3030

This organization believes that cigarette advertising is harmful to society. It contends that such advertising recruits new smokers, many of them teenagers. The Society publishes *Cancer—A Journal of the American Cancer Society* and *World Smoking and Health*.

Committee To Protect Journalists (CPJ)
36 W. 44th St.
New York, NY 10036
(212) 944-7216

The Committee works on behalf of journalists around the world whose human and professional rights have been violated. It believes that there is a growing effort by governments to limit the ability of foreign correspondents and local journalists to practice their profession. It publishes *Update*, bimonthly.

First Amendment Congress
c/o Jean H. Otto
Rocky Mountain News
400 W. Colfax
Denver, CO 80204
(303) 892-5478

The Congress believes that a free press is not the special prerogative of print and broadcast journalists but a basic right that assures a responsive government. It works to establish a dialogue between the press and people across the country, to encourage better education in schools about the rights and responsibilities of citizenship, and to obtain broader support from the public against all attempts by government to restrict the citizen's right to information. It publishes a newsletter, brochures, and booklets.

Foundation for American Communications
3383 Barham Blvd.
Los Angeles, CA 90068
(213) 851-7372

The Foundation seeks to improve mutual understanding between major American institutions and the news media. Its publications include the magazine *The Journalist* as well as many discussion papers on current public policy issues.

Freedom To Read Foundation (FTRF)
50 E. Huron St.
Chicago, IL 60611
(312) 944-6780

The Foundation promotes the public right of access to libraries, the right of librarians to make available to the public any creative work legally acquired, and to counter censorship in libraries. It publishes *News*, quarterly.

The Media Institute
3017 M St. NW
Washington, DC 20007
(202) 298-7512

The Institute conducts research into the legal, economic, and political aspects of the media and its role in American society. Its publications include *Media Institute Forum*, published quarterly, and *Business and the Media*, published three times a year. The Institute also has books, studies, and monographs available.

Media Network
208 W. 13th St.
New York, NY 10011
(212) 620-0877

The objectives of the organization are to increase public awareness of the ways in which film, videotape, and slideshow media define and influence people's lives.

It presents alternative ideas and progressive views that it believes are not offered by mass media to educate and effect social change. Its goal is to improve the quality and broaden the audience of independently produced media. The Network publishes *Guide to Disarmament Media, Guide to Media on Reproductive Rights, Mobilizing Media,* and other media manuals and guides.

Morality in Media, Inc.
475 Riverside Dr.
New York, NY 10115
(212) 870-3222

This group opposes pornography in the media and encourages more vigorous enforcement of obscenity laws. It does not believe in censorship or prior restraint by the government. It publishes *Morality in Media Newsletter, Hill-Link Report of the Presidential Commission on Obscenity and Pornography,* and legal publications.

National Association for Better Broadcasting (NABB)
7918 Naylor Ave.
Los Angeles, CA 90045
(213) 641-4903

The Association surveys programs, commercials, and station programming. It works for laws and regulations that will improve broadcasting. It publishes *Better Radio and Television,* quarterly, and *You Own More than Your Set! — Broadcasting Law and the Consumer.*

National Beer Wholesalers' Association (NBWA)
5205 Leesburg Pike, Suite 505
Falls Church, VA 22041
(703) 578-4300

The Association is a body of independent wholesalers affiliated with the malt beverage industry. It opposes restrictions and censorship of alcohol advertisements in the media. It publishes the monthly *Washington Update.*

National Coalition Against Censorship (NCAC)
132 W. 43rd St.
New York, NY 10036
(212) 944-9899

The Coalition opposes all forms of censorship. It publishes *Censorship News,* quarterly, and *Books on Trial: A Survey on Recent Cases,* annually.

National Coalition on Television Violence (NCTV)
PO Box 2157
Champaign, IL 61820
(217) 384-1920

The Coalition is an educational and research organization that is committed to decreasing the amount of violence in television and film. It publishes *Film Review Weekly* and *News,* eight times yearly, in addition to research materials.

National Council for Families and Television (NCFT)
20 Nassau St., Suite 200
Princeton, NJ 08542
(609) 921-3639

The group's purpose is to enhance family life by encouraging quality family-oriented prime time television programs. Publications include *NCFT Information Service,* monthly, and *Television and Families,* quarterly.

National Federation for Decency (NFD)
PO Drawer 2440
Tupelo, MS 38803
(601) 844-5036

The Federation promotes "the biblical ethic of decency in American society with a primary emphasis on television." It urges viewers to write letters to networks and sponsors, protesting shows that promote "violence, immorality, profanity and vulgarity." It publishes a monthly newsletter.

Parents' Music Resource Center (PMRC)
1500 Arlington Blvd.
Arlington, VA 22209
(703) 527-9466

The Center believes record companies should maintain a music ratings system that would alert parents and children to lyrics describing explicit sex, violence, and drug abuse. It publishes *The Record*, a quarterly magazine.

Reporters' Committee for Freedom of the Press (RCFP)
800 18th St. NW, Suite 300
Washington, DC 20006
(202) 466-6312

The Committee is devoted to protecting the rights of the press and to upholding the First Amendment. It studies how subpoenas of reporters' notes affects their ability to gather news from confidential sources. It opposes closing criminal justice proceedings to the public and press. RCFP publishes *News Media Update*, biweekly, and *News Media and the Law*, quarterly.

Silha Center for the Study of Media Ethics and Law
School of Journalism and Mass Communication
University of Minnesota
405 Murphy Hall, 206 Church St.
Minneapolis, MN 55455-0418
(612) 625-9038

The Center analyzes the roles and responsibilities of the media in democratic society. The Center publishes the annual Silha lectures, a guide to the archives of the National News Council, and a bibliography of books and articles.

Society for the Eradication of Television (SET)
Box 1124
Albuquerque, NM 87103
(505) 247-3245

The Society encourages people to remove televisions from their homes. It believes television retards the inner life of human beings, destroys human interaction, squanders time, and makes viewers addicted to television. The Society publishes the quarterly newsletter *SET Free*.

Tobacco Institute (TI)
1875 Eye St. NW, Suite 800
Washington, DC 20006
(202) 457-4800

The Institute works for public understanding of the tobacco industry and its place in the nation's economy. It is opposed to censoring cigarette advertising and questions the link between cigarette smoking and cancer. It has several publications, including the quarterly *Tobacco Observer*.

Bibliography of Books

Warren K. Agee, Phillip H. Ault, and Edwin Emery — *Maincurrents in Mass Communications*. San Francisco: Harper and Row, 1986.

J. Herbert Altschull — *Agents of Power: The Role of the News Media in Human Affairs*. New York: Longman, 1984.

American Society of Newspaper Editors and the American Newspaper Publishers Association Foundation — *Free Press and Fair Trial*. Washington, DC: ANDA Foundation, 1987.

F. Christopher Arterton — *Media Politics*. Lexington, MA: Lexington Books, 1984.

Robert Atwan, Bobby Orton, and William Vesterman — *American Mass Media*. New York: Random House, 1986.

Shirley Biagi — *News Talk I*. Belmont, CA: Wadsworth, 1987.

Shirley Biagi — *News Talk II*. Belmont, CA: Wadsworth, 1987.

Jennings Bryant and Dolf Zillmann — *Perspectives on Media Effects*. Hillsdale, NJ: Lawrence Erlbaum Associates, 1986.

Don Fry, ed. — *Believing the News*. St. Petersburg, FL: The Poynter Institute for Media Studies, 1985.

Tom Goldstein — *The News at any Cost*. New York: Simon and Schuster, 1985.

H. Eugene Goodwin — *Groping for Ethics in Journalism*. Ames, IA: Iowa State University Press, 1983.

Tipper Gore — *Raising PG Kids in an X-rated Society*. Nashville, TN: Abingdon Press, 1987.

Doris A. Graber — *Mass Media and American Politics*. Washington, DC: Congressional Quarterly, 1984.

Doris A. Graber — *Processing the News: How People Tame the Information Tide*. New York: Longman, 1984.

Ray Eldon Hiebert and Carol Reuss, eds. — *Impact of the Mass Media*. New York: Longman, 1985.

John L. Hulteng — *The Messenger's Motive: Ethical Problems of the News Media*. Englewood Cliffs, NJ: Prentice-Hall, 1985.

Richard Joslyn — *Mass Media and Elections*. Reading, MA: Addison-Wesley, 1984.

Don Kowet — *A Matter of Honor*. New York: Macmillan Books, 1984.

Michael Kronenwetter — *Free Press v. Fair Trial*. New York: Franklin Watts, 1986.

William Leiss, Stephen Kline, and Sut Jhally — *Social Communication in Advertising*. New York: Macmillan, 1986.

S. Robert Lichter, Stanley Rothman, and Linda S. Richter — *The Media Elite*. Bethesda, MD: Adler and Adler, 1986.

Martin Linsky	*Impact: How the Press Affects Federal Policymaking.* New York: W.W. Norton & Company, 1986.
Shearon Lowery and Melvin L. De Fleur	*Milestones in Mass Communication Research.* New York: Longman, 1987.
Frank McCulloch, ed.	*Drawing the Line.* Washington, DC: American Association of Newspaper Editors, 1984.
The Media Institute	*Media Abuse: Rights and Remedies.* Washington, DC: The Media Institute, 1983.
W. Russell Neuman	*The Paradox of Mass Politics.* Cambridge, MA: Harvard University Press, 1986.
John O'Toole	*The Trouble with Advertising.* New York: Times Books, 1985.
Lucas A. Powe Jr.	*American Broadcasting and the First Amendment.* Berkeley, CA: University of California Press, 1987.
Elayne Rapping	*The Looking Glass World of Nonfiction Television.* Boston: South End Press, 1987.
Ford Rowan	*Broadcast Fairness.* New York: Longman, 1984.
Michael Schudson	*Advertising, The Uneasy Persuasion.* New York: Basic Books, 1984.
David Shaw	*Press Watch.* New York: Macmillan, 1984.
Bruce M. Swain	*Reporters' Ethics.* Ames, IA: Iowa State University Press, 1978.
Kenneth W. Thompson, ed.	*The Media.* New York: University Press of America, 1985.
Donald F. Ungurait, Thomas W. Bohn, and Ray Eldon Hiebert, eds.	*Media Now.* New York: Longman, 1985.
Edward Jay Whetmore	*Mediamerica*, third edition. Belmont, CA: Wadsworth, 1987.
Clint C. Wilson II and Felix Gutierrez	*Minorities and the Media.* Beverly Hills, CA: Sage Publications, 1985.
Charles R. Wright	*Mass Communication.* New York: Random House, 1986.
Melvyn Bernard Zerman	*Taking on the Press.* New York: Thomas Y. Crowell, 1986.

233

Index